The Builder of Modern India

Rabindranath Tagore

The Builder of Modern India
Rabindranath Tagore

Dr. Madhubala Sinha

Vinod Book Center
Delhi–110053

ISBN : 978-93-5588-007-6

Publishers : **Vinod Book Center**
L-20/13, Ist Floor, Gali No. 5
Shivaji Marg, Kartar Nagar
Delhi–110053

First Edition : 2023

Price : 595.00

Type Setting : Priyanka Graphics, Delhi

Printers : Shiv Shakti Printers, Delhi–110032

The Builder of Modern India Rabindranath Tagore
(in English) *By* **Dr. Madhubala Sinha**

Contents

1. **Introduction** 7
- Early Life
- Santiniketan
- Twilight Years
- Travels
- Works
- Novels and Non-fiction
- Music and Artwork
- Theatrical Pieces
- Short Stories
- Poetry
- Political Views
- Impact and Legacy
- Life of Rabindranath Tagore (1861–1901)
- Family Background
- Childhood (1861–1878)
- Schooling in England
- Shelaidaha
- Life of Rabindranath Tagore (1901–1932)
- Santiniketan
- Life of Rabindranath Tagore (1932–1941)
- Illness of 1937-1941
- Chokher Bali
- Plot Summary
- Critical Acclaim
- Adaptations
- Poetry
- Writing on the Screen: Satyajit Ray's Adaptation of Tagore

2. Tagore and His India **40**
- Voice of Bengal
- The Mystic
- Confluence of Cultures
- Abode of Peace
- Gandhi and Tagore
- East and West
- God and Others
- Reasoning in Freedom
- Celibacy and Personal Life
- Educational Ideas
- Science and the People
- Nationalism and Colonialism
- Critique of Patriotism
- Admiration and Criticism of Japan
- International Concerns
- Education and Freedom
- India Today
- On Cultural Separation
- The Parrot's Tale

3. The Sources of Tagore's Poetic Imagination **146**
- The Fundamental Confusion
- Religion
- Later Reactions
- Prose and Paintings
- Politics and Nationalism
- The Man Himself

4. Rabindra Sangeet **164**
- Influence and Legacy
- Singers of Rabindrasangeet
- Teachers of Rabindrasangeet
- Ekla Chalo Re
- Lyrics
- Tagore's English Translation
- In Popular Culture

5. Selected Quotations of Rabindranath Tagore **183**

1

Introduction

Rabindranath Tagore (7 May 1861 – 7 August 1941), also known by the sobriquet Gurudev, was a Bengali poet, Brahmo Samaj philosopher, visual artist, playwright, novelist, and composer whose works reshaped Bengali literature and music in the late 19th and early 20th centuries. He became Asia's first Nobel laureate when he won the 1913 Nobel Prize in Literature.

A Pirali Bengali Brahmin from Calcutta, Tagore first wrote poems at the age of eight. At the age of sixteen, he published his first substantial poetry under the pseudonym *Bhanushingho* ("Sun Lion") and wrote his first short stories and dramas in 1877. His home schooling, life in Shilaidaha, and travels made Tagore a nonconformist and pragmatist.

Tagore strongly protested against the British Raj and gave his support to the Indian Independence Movement and Mahatma Gandhi. Tagore's life was tragic—he lost virtually his entire family and was devastated to witness Bengal's decline—but his life's work endured, in the form of his poetry and the institution he founded, Visva-Bharati University.

Tagore wrote novels, short stories, songs, dance-dramas, and essays on political and personal topics. *Gitanjali* (*Song Offerings*), *Gora* (*Fair-Faced*), and *Ghare-Baire* (*The Home and the World*) are among his best-known works. His verse, short stories, and novels, which often exhibited rhythmic lyricism, colloquial language, meditative naturalism, and philosophical contemplation, received worldwide acclaim.

Tagore was also a cultural reformer and polymath who modernised Bengali art by rejecting strictures binding it to classical Indian forms. Two songs from his *rabindrasangeet* canon are now the national anthems of Bangladesh and India: the *Amar Shonar Bangla* and the *Jana Gana Mana*.

Early Life

Tagore (nicknamed "Rabi") was born the youngest of thirteen surviving children in the Jorasanko mansion in Calcutta (now Kolkata, India) of parents Debendranath Tagore and Sarada Devi. After undergoing his *upanayan* (the *sacred thread* ceremony, a coming-of-age rite) at age eleven, Tagore and his father left Calcutta on 14 February 1873 to tour India for several months, visiting his father's Santiniketan estate and Amritsar before reaching the Himalayan hill station of Dalhousie. There, Tagore read biographies, studied history, astronomy, modern science, and Sanskrit, and examined the classical poetry of Kalidsa. In 1877, he rose to notability when he composed several works, including a long poem set in the Maithili style pioneered by Vidyapati. As a joke, he maintained that these were the lost works of Bhnusi Cha, a newly discovered 17th-century Vaicgava poet. He also wrote "Bhikharini" (1877; "The Beggar Woman"—the Bengali language's first short story) and *Sandhya Sangit* (1882) —including the famous poem "Nirjharer Swapnabhanga" ("The Rousing of the Waterfall").

Seeking to become a barrister, Tagore enrolled at a public school in Brighton, England in 1878. He studied law at University College London, but returned to Bengal in 1880 without a degree. On 9 December 1883 he married Mrinalini Devi (born Bhabatarini, 1873–1902); they had five children, two of whom later died before reaching adulthood. In 1890, Tagore began managing his family's estates in Shilaidaha, a region now in Bangladesh; he was joined by his wife and children in 1898. Known as "Zamindar Babu", Tagore travelled across the vast estate while living out of the family's luxurious barge, the *Padma*, to collect (mostly token) rents and bless villagers; in return, appreciative villagers held feasts in his honour. These years, which composed Tagore's *Sadhana* period (1891–1895; named for one of Tagore's magazines), were among his most fecund. More than half the stories of the three-volume and eighty-four-story *Galpaguchchha* written. With irony and emotional weight, they depicted a wide range of Bengali lifestyles, particularly village life.

Santiniketan

In 1901, Tagore left Shilaidaha and moved to Santiniketan (West Bengal) to found an ashram, which would grow to include a marble-floored prayer hall ("The Mandir"), an experimental school, groves of trees, gardens, and a library. There, Tagore's wife and two of his children died. His father died on 19 January 1905, and he began receiving monthly payments as part of his inheritance. He received additional income from the Maharaja of Tripura, sales of his family's jewellery, his seaside bungalow in Puri, and mediocre royalties (Rs. 2,000) from his works.

These works gained him a large following among Bengali and foreign readers alike, and he published such works as *Naivedya* (1901) and *Kheya* (1906) while translating his poems into free verse. On 14 November 1913, Tagore learned that he had won the 1913 Nobel Prize in Literature. According to the Swedish Academy, it was given due to the idealistic and—for Western readers—accessible nature of a small body of his translated material, including the 1912 *Gitanjali: Song Offerings*. In 1915, Tagore also accepted knighthood from the British Crown.

In 1921, Tagore and agricultural economist Leonard Elmhirst set up the Institute for Rural Reconstruction (which Tagore later renamed Shriniketan—"Abode of Peace") in Surul, a village near the ashram at Santiniketan. Through it, Tagore sought to provide an alternative to Gandhi's symbol- and protest-based *Swaraj* movement, which he denounced. He recruited scholars, donors, and officials from many countries to help the Institute use schooling to "free village[s] from the shackles of helplessness and ignorance" by "vitaliz[ing] knowledge". In the early 1930s, he also grew more concerned about India's "abnormal caste consciousness" and untouchability, lecturing on its evils, writing poems and dramas with untouchable protagonists, and appealing to authorities at the Guruvayoor Temple to admit Dalits.

Twilight Years

In his last decade, Tagore remained in the public limelight, publicly upbraiding Gandhi for stating that a massive 15 January 1934 earthquake in Bihar constituted divine retribution for the subjugation of Dalits. He also mourned the incipient socioeconomic decline of Bengal and the endemic poverty of Calcutta; he detailed the latter in an unrhymed hundred-line poem whose technique of searing double-vision would foreshadow Satyajit Ray's film *Apur Sansar*. Tagore also compiled fifteen volumes of writings, including the prose-poems works *Punashcha* (1932), *Shes Saptak* (1935), and *Patraput* (1936). He continued his experimentations by developing prose-songs and dance-dramas, including *Chitrangada* (1914), *Shyama* (1939), and *Chandalika* (1938), and wrote the novels *Dui Bon* (1933), *Malancha* (1934), and *Char Adhyay* (1934). Tagore took an interest in science in his last years, writing *Visva-Parichay* (a collection of essays) in 1937. His exploration of biology, physics, and astronomy impacted his poetry, which often contained extensive naturalism that underscored his respect for scientific laws. He also wove the process of science (including narratives of scientists) into many stories contained in such volumes as *Se* (1937), *Tin Sangi* (1940), and *Galpasalpa* (1941).

Tagore's last four years were marked by chronic pain and two long periods of illness. These began when Tagore lost consciousness in late 1937; he remained comatose and near death for an extended period. This was followed three years later in late 1940 by a similar spell, from which he never recovered. The poetry Tagore wrote in these years is among his finest, and is distinctive for its preoccupation with death. After extended suffering, Tagore died on 7 August 1941 (22 Shravan 1348) in an upstairs room of the Jorasanko mansion in which he was raised; his death anniversary is still mourned in public functions held across the Bengali-speaking world.

Travels

Owing to his notable wanderlust, between 1878 and 1932, Tagore visited more than thirty countries on five continents; many of these trips were crucial in familiarising non-Indian audiences to his works and spreading his political ideas. In 1912, he took a sheaf of his translated works to England, where they impressed missionary and Gandhi protege Charles F. Andrews, Anglo-Irish poet William Butler Yeats, Ezra Pound, Robert Bridges, Ernest Rhys, Thomas Sturge Moore, and others. Indeed, Yeats wrote the preface to the English translation of Gitanjali, while Andrews joined Tagore at Santiniketan. On 10 November 1912, Tagore toured the United States and the United Kingdom, staying in Butterton, Staffordshire with Andrews' clergymen friends. From 3 May 1916 until April 1917, Tagore went on lecturing circuits in Japan and the United States, during which he denounced nationalism—particularly that of the Japanese and Americans. He also wrote the essay "Nationalism in India", attracting both derision and praise (the latter from pacifists, including Romain Rolland). Shortly after returning to India, the 63-year-old Tagore visited Peru at the invitation of the Peruvian government, and took the opportunity to visit Mexico as well.

Both governments pledged donations of $100,000 to the school at Shantiniketan (Visva-Bharati) in commemoration of his visits. A week after his November 6, 1924 arrival in Buenos Aires, Argentina, an ill Tagore moved into the Villa Miralrío at the behest of Victoria Ocampo. He left for India in January 1925. On 30 May 1926, Tagore reached Naples, Italy; he met fascist dictator Benito Mussolini in Rome the next day. Their initially warm rapport lasted until Tagore spoke out against Mussolini on 20 July 1926.

On 14 July 1927, Tagore and two companions began a four-month tour of Southeast Asia, visiting Bali, Java, Kuala Lumpur, Malacca, Penang, Siam, and Singapore. Tagore's travelogues from the tour were collected into the work "Jatri". In early 1930 he left Bengal for a nearly year-long tour of Europe and the United States. Once he returned to the UK, while his paintings were being exhibited in Paris and London, he stayed at a Friends settlement in Birmingham. There, he wrote his Hibbert Lectures for the University of Oxford (which dealt with the "idea of the humanity of our God, or the divinity of Man the Eternal") and spoke at London's annual Quaker gathering. There (addressing relations between the British and Indians, a topic he would grapple with over the next two years), Tagore spoke of a "dark chasm of aloofness". He later visited Aga Khan III, stayed at Dartington Hall, then toured Denmark, Switzerland, and Germany from June to mid-September 1930, then the Soviet Union. Lastly, in April 1932, Tagore—who was acquainted with the legends and works of the Persian mystic Hafez—was invited as a personal guest of Shah Reza Shah Pahlavi of Iran. Such extensive travels allowed Tagore to interact with many notable contemporaries, including Henri Bergson, Albert Einstein, Robert Frost, Thomas Mann, George Bernard Shaw, H.G. Wells and Romain Rolland. Tagore's last travels abroad, including visits to Persia and Iraq (in 1932) and Ceylon in 1933, only sharpened his opinions regarding human divisions and nationalism.

Works

Tagore's Bengali-language initials are worked into this "Ra-Tha" wooden seal, which bears close stylistic similarity to designs used in traditional Haida carvings. Tagore often embellished his manuscripts with such art. (Dyson 2001)

Tagore's literary reputation is disproportionately influenced by regard for his poetry; however, he also wrote novels, essays, short stories, travelogues, dramas, and thousands of songs. Of Tagore's prose, his short stories are perhaps most highly regarded; indeed, he is credited with originating the Bengali-language version of the genre. His works are frequently noted for their rhythmic, optimistic, and lyrical nature. Such stories mostly borrow from deceptively simple subject matter: the lives of ordinary people.

Novels and Non-fiction

Tagore wrote eight novels and four novellas, including *Chaturanga*, *Shesher Kobita*, *Char Odhay*, and *Noukadubi*. *Ghare Baire* (*The Home and the World*)—through the lens of the idealistic *zamindar* protagonist Nikhil—excoriates rising Indian nationalism, terrorism, and religious zeal in the *Swadeshi* movement; a frank expression of Tagore's conflicted sentiments, it emerged out of a 1914 bout of depression. Indeed, the novel bleakly ends with Hindu-Muslim sectarian violence and Nikhil's being (probably mortally) wounded. In some sense, *Gora* shares the same theme, raising controversial questions regarding the Indian identity. As with *Ghore Baire*, matters of self-identity (*jti*), personal freedom, and religion are developed in the context of a family story and love triangle. Another powerful story is *Yogayog* (*Nexus*), where the heroine Kumudini—bound by the ideals of *Shiva-Sati*, exemplified by Dkshyani—is torn between her pity for the sinking fortunes of her progressive and compassionate elder brother and his foil: her exploitative, rakish, and patriarchical husband. In it, Tagore demonstrates his feminist leanings, using *pathos* to depict the plight and ultimate demise of Bengali women trapped by pregnancy, duty, and family honour; simultaneously, he treats the decline of Bengal's landed oligarchy.

Other novels were more uplifting: *Shesher Kobita* (translated twice—*Last Poem* and *Farewell Song*) is his most lyrical novel, with poems and rhythmic passages written by the main character (a poet). It also contains elements of satire and postmodernism; stock characters gleefully attack the reputation of an old, outmoded, oppressively renowned poet who, incidentally, goes by the name of Rabindranath Tagore. Though his novels remain among the least-appreciated of his works, they have been given renewed attention via film adaptations by such directors as Satyajit Ray; these include *Chokher Bali* and *Ghare Baire*; many have soundtracks featuring selections from Tagore's own *rabindrasangit*. Tagore wrote many non-fiction books, writing on topics ranging from Indian history to linguistics. Aside from autobiographical works, his travelogues, essays, and lectures were compiled into several volumes, including *Iurop Jatrir Patro* (*Letters from Europe*) and *Manusher Dhormo* (*The Religion of Man*).

Music and Artwork

Tagore was a prolific musician and painter, writing around 2,230 songs. They compose *rabindrasangit* now an integral part of Bengali culture. Tagore's music is inseparable from his literature, most of which—poems or parts of novels, stories, or plays alike—became lyrics for his songs. Primarily influenced by the *thumri* style of Hindustani classical music, they ran the entire gamut of human emotion, ranging from his early dirge-like Brahmo devotional hymns to quasi-erotic compositions. They emulated the tonal colour of classical *ragas* to varying extents. Though at times his songs mimicked a given raga's melody and rhythm faithfully, he also blended elements of different ragas to create innovative works.

For Bengalis, their appeal, stemming from the combination of emotive strength and beauty described as surpassing even Tagore's poetry, was such that the *Modern Review* observed that "[t]here is in Bengal no cultured home where Rabindranath's songs are not sung or at least attempted to be sung ... Even illiterate villagers sing his songs". Music critic Arthur Strangways of *The Observer* first introduced non-Bengalis to *rabindrasangeet* with his book *The Music of Hindostan*, which described it as a "vehicle of a personality ... [that] go behind this or that system of music to that beauty of sound which all systems put out their hands to seize." Among them are Bangladesh's national anthem *Amar Shonar Bangla* and India's national anthem *Jana Gana Mana*; Tagore thus became the only person ever to have written the national anthems of two nations. In turn, *rabindrasangeet* influenced the styles of such musicians as sitar maestro Vilayat Khan, and the *sarodiyas* Buddhadev Dasgupta and Amjad Ali Khan.

At age sixty, Tagore took up drawing and painting; successful exhibitions of his many works—which made a debut appearance in Paris upon encouragement by artists he met in the south of France—were held throughout Europe. Tagore—who likely exhibited protanopia ("color blindness"), or partial lack of (red-green, in Tagore's case) colour discernment—painted in a style characterised by peculiarities in aesthetics and colouring schemes.

Nevertheless, Tagore took to emulating numerous styles, including that of craftwork by the Malanggan people of northern New Ireland, Haida carvings from the west coast of Canada (British Columbia), and woodcuts by Max Pechstein. Tagore also had an artist's eye for his own handwriting, embellishing the scribbles, cross-outs, and word layouts in his manuscripts with simple artistic leitmotifs, including simple rhythmic designs.

Theatrical Pieces

Tagore's experience in theatre began at age sixteen, when he played the lead role in his brother Jyotirindranath's adaptation of Molière's *Le Bourgeois Gentilhomme*. At age twenty, he wrote his first drama-opera— *Valmiki Pratibha* (*The Genius of Valmiki*)—which describes how the bandit Valmiki reforms his ethos, is blessed by Saraswati, and composes the *Ramayana*.

Through it, Tagore vigorously explores a wide range of dramatic styles and emotions, including usage of revamped *kirtans* and adaptation of traditional English and Irish folk melodies as drinking songs. Another notable play, *Dak Ghar* (*The Post Office*), describes how a child—striving to escape his stuffy confines—ultimately "fall[s] asleep" (which suggests his physical death). A story with worldwide appeal (it received rave reviews in Europe), *Dak Ghar* dealt with death as, in Tagore's words, "spiritual freedom" from "the world of hoarded wealth and certified creeds".

His other works—emphasizing fusion of lyrical flow and emotional rhythm tightly focused on a core idea—were unlike previous Bengali dramas. His works sought to articulate, in Tagore's words, "the play of feeling and not of action". In 1890 he wrote *Visarjan* (*Sacrifice*), regarded as his finest drama. The Bengali-language originals included intricate subplots and extended monologues. Later, his dramas probed more philosophical and allegorical themes; these included *Dak Ghar*. Another is Tagore's *Chandalika* (*Untouchable Girl*), which was modeled on an ancient Buddhist legend describing how Ananda—the Gautama Buddha's disciple—asks water of an *Adivasi* ("untouchable") girl. Lastly, among his most famous dramas is *Raktakaravi* (*Red Oleanders*), which tells of a kleptocratic king who enriches himself by forcing his subjects to mine. The heroine, Nandini, eventually rallies the common people to destroy these symbols of subjugation. Tagore's other plays include *Chitrangada*, *Raja*, and *Mayar Khela*. Dance dramas based on Tagore's plays are commonly referred to as *rabindra nritya natyas*.

Short Stories

Tagore's "Sadhana" period, comprising the four years from 1891 to 1895, was named for one of Tagore's magazines. This period was among Tagore's most fecund, yielding more than half the stories contained in the three-volume *Galpaguchchha*, which itself is a collection of eighty-four stories.

Such stories usually showcase Tagore's reflections upon his surroundings, on modern and fashionable ideas, and on interesting mind puzzles (which Tagore was fond of testing his intellect with). Tagore typically associated his earliest stories (such as those of the "*Sadhana*" period) with an exuberance of vitality and spontaneity; these characteristics were intimately connected with Tagore's life in the common villages of, among others, Patisar, Shajadpur, and Shilaida while managing the Tagore family's vast landholdings. There, he beheld the lives of India's poor and common people; Tagore thereby took to examining their lives with a penetrative depth and feeling that was singular in Indian literature up to that point.

In "The Fruitseller from Kabul", Tagore speaks in first person as town-dweller and novelist who chances upon the Afghani seller. He attempts to distil the sense of longing felt by those long trapped in the mundane and hardscrabble confines of Indian urban life, giving play to dreams of a different existence in the distant and wild mountains: "There were autumn mornings, the time of year when kings of old went forth to conquest; and I, never stirring from my little corner in Calcutta, would let my mind wander over the whole world. At the very name of another country, my heart would go out to it ... I would fall to weaving a network of dreams: the mountains, the glens, the forest .... ". Many of the other *Galpaguchchha* stories were written in Tagore's *Sabuj Patra* period (1914–1917; also named for one of Tagore's magazines).

Tagore's *Golpoguchchho* (*Bunch of Stories*) remains among Bengali literature's most popular fictional works, providing subject matter for many successful films and theatrical plays. Satyajit Ray's film *Charulata* was based upon Tagore's controversial novella, *Nastanirh* (*The Broken Nest*). In *Atithi* (also made into a film), the young Brahmin boy Tarapada shares a boat ride with a village zamindar.

The boy reveals that he has run away from home, only to wander around ever since. Taking pity, the zamindar adopts him and ultimately arranges his marriage to the zamindar's own daughter. However, the night before the wedding, Tarapada runs off—again. *Strir Patra* (*The Letter from the Wife*) is among Bengali literature's earliest depictions of the bold emancipation of women. The heroine Mrinal, the wife of a typical patriarchical Bengali middle class man, writes a letter while she is traveling (which constitutes the whole story). It details the pettiness of her life and struggles; she finally declares that she will not return to her husband's home with the statement *Amio bachbo. Ei bachlum* ("And I shall live. Here, I live").

In *Haimanti*, Tagore takes on the institution of Hindu marriage, describing the dismal lifelessness of married Bengali women, hypocrisies plaguing the Indian middle classes, and how Haimanti, a sensitive young woman, must—due to her sensitiveness and free spirit—sacrifice her life. In the last passage, Tagore directly attacks the Hindu custom of glorifying Sita's attempted self-immolation as a means of appeasing her husband Rama's doubts. Tagore also examines Hindu-Muslim tensions in *Musalmani Didi*, which in many ways embodies the essence of Tagore's humanism. On the other hand, *Darpaharan* exhibits Tagore's self-consciousness, describing a young man harboring literary ambitions. Though he loves his wife, he wishes to stifle her own literary career, deeming it unfeminine. Tagore himself, in his youth, seems to have harboured similar ideas about women. *Darpaharan* depicts the final humbling of the man via his acceptance of his wife's talents. As many other Tagore stories, *Jibito o Mrito* provides the Bengalis with one of their more widely used epigrams: *Kadombini moriya proman korilo she more nai* ("Kadombini died, thereby proved that she hadn't").

Poetry

Tagore's poetry—which varied in style from classical formalism to the comic, visionary, and ecstatic—proceeds out a lineage established by 15th- and 16th-century VaicGava poets. Tagore was also influenced by the mysticism of the *rishi*-authors who—including Vyasa—wrote the Upanishads, the Bhakta-Sufi mystic Kabir, and Ramprasad. Yet Tagore's poetry became most innovative and mature after his exposure to rural Bengal's folk music, which included ballads sung by Bul folk singers—especially the bard Llan Zh. These—which were rediscovered and popularised by Tagore—resemble 19th-century Kartbhaj hymns that emphasize inward divinity and rebellion against religious and social orthodoxy.

During his Shilaidaha years, his poems took on a lyrical quality, speaking via the *maner manus* (the Bauls' "man within the heart") or meditating upon the *jivan devata* ("living God within"). This figure thus sought connection with divinity through appeal to nature and the emotional interplay of human drama. Tagore used such techniques in his Bhnusi Cha poems (which chronicle the romanticism between Radha and Krishna), which he repeatedly revised over the course of seventy years.

Later, Tagore responded to the (mostly) crude emergence of modernism and realism in Bengali literature by writing experimental works in the 1930s. Examples works include *Africa* and *Camalia*, which are among the better known of his latter poems. He also occasionally wrote poems using *Shadhu Bhasha* (a Sanskritised dialect of Bengali); later, he began using *Cholti Bhasha* (a more popular dialect).

Other notable works include *Manasi*, *Sonar Tori* (*Golden Boat*), *Balaka* (*Wild Geese*—the title being a metaphor for migrating souls), and *Purobi*. *Sonar Tori*'s most famous poem—dealing with the ephemeral nature of life and achievement—goes by the same name; it ends with the haunting phrase ("*Shunno nodir tire rohinu poi / Jaha chhilo loe gêlo shonar tori*"—"all I had achieved was carried off on the golden boat—only I was left behind."). Internationally, *Gitanjali* is Tagore's best-known collection, winning him his Nobel Prize.

Political Views

Marked complexities characterise Tagore's political views. He criticised European imperialism and supported Indian nationalists and although he himself vehemently denied it at the time, the evidence produced during the Hindu-German Conspiracy trial, as well as some later accounts, he was aware of the conspiracy and even interviewed the then Japanese premier Count Terauchi and former premier Count Okuma on behalf of the conspirators to try and enlist Japanese support. However, he also lampooned the Swadeshi movement, denouncing it in "The Cult of the Charka", an acrid 1925 essay. Instead, he emphasized self-help and intellectual uplift of the masses, stating that British imperialism was not a primary evil, but instead a "political symptom of our social disease", urging Indians to accept that "there can be no question of blind revolution, but of steady and purposeful education".

Such views inevitably enraged many, placing his life in danger: during his stay in a San Francisco hotel in late 1916, Tagore narrowly escaped assassination by Indian expatriates. The plot failed only because the would-be assassins fell into argument. Yet Tagore wrote songs lionizing the Indian independence movement and renounced his knighthood in protest against the 1919 Jallianwala Bagh Massacre. Two of Tagore's more politically charged compositions, "Chitto Jetha Bhayshunyo" ("Where the Mind is Without Fear") and "Ekla Chalo Re" ("If They Answer Not to Thy Call, Walk Alone"), gained mass appeal, with the latter favoured by Gandhi. Despite his tumultuous relations with Gandhi, Tagore was key in resolving a Gandhi-Ambedkar dispute involving separate electorates for untouchables, ending Gandhi's fast "unto death".

Tagore also criticised orthodox (rote-oriented) education, lampooning it in the short story "The Parrot's Training", where a bird—which ultimately dies—is caged by tutors and force-fed pages torn from books. These views led Tagore—while visiting Santa Barbara, California on 11 October 1917—to conceive of a new type of university, desiring to "make [his ashram at] Santiniketan the connecting thread between India and the world ... [and] a world centre for the study of humanity ...

somewhere beyond the limits of nation and geography." The school—which he named Visva-Bharati—had its foundation stone laid on 22 December 1918; it was later inaugurated on 22 December 1921.

Here, Tagore implemented a *brahmacharya* pedagogical structure employing *gurus* to provide individualised guidance for pupils. Tagore worked hard to fundraise for and staff the school, even contributing all of his Nobel Prize monies. Tagore's duties as steward and mentor at Santiniketan kept him busy; he taught classes in mornings and wrote the students' textbooks in afternoons and evenings. Tagore also fundraised extensively for the school in Europe and the U.S. between 1919 and 1921.

Impact and Legacy

Tagore's post-death impact can be felt through the many festivals held worldwide in his honour—examples include the annual Bengali festival/celebration of *Kabipranam* (Tagore's birthday anniversary), the annual Tagore Festival held in Urbana, Illinois in the United States, the *Rabindra Path Parikrama* walking pilgrimages leading from Calcutta to Shantiniketan, and ceremonial recitals of Tagore's poetry held on important anniversaries.

This legacy is most palpable in Bengali culture, ranging from language and arts to history and politics; indeed, Nobel laureate Amartya Sen noted that even for modern Bengalis, Tagore was a "towering figure", being a "deeply relevant and manysided contemporary thinker". Tagore's collected Bengali-language writings—the 1939 *Rab+ndra Racanval+*—is also canonized as one of Bengal's greatest cultural treasures, while Tagore himself has been proclaimed "the greatest poet India has produced".

Tagore was famed throughout much of Europe, North America, and East Asia. He was key in founding Dartington Hall School, a progressive coeducational institution; in Japan, he influenced such figures as Nobel laureate Yasunari Kawabata. Tagore's works were widely translated into English, Dutch, German, Spanish, and other European languages by

Czech indologist Vincent Slesny, French Nobel laureate André Gide, Russian poet Anna Akhmatova, and others. In the United States, Tagore's popular lecturing circuits (especially those between 1916–1917) were widely attended and acclaimed. Nevertheless, several controversies involving Tagore resulted in a decline in his popularity in Japan and North America after the late 1920s, contributing to his "near total eclipse" outside of Bengal.

Tagore, through Spanish translations of his works, also influenced leading figures of Spanish literature, including Chileans Pablo Neruda and Gabriela Mistral, Mexican writer Octavio Paz, and Spaniards José Ortega y Gasset, Zenobia Camprubí, and Juan Ramón Jiménez. Between 1914 and 1922, the Jiménez-Camprubí spouses translated no less than twenty-two of Tagore's books from English into Spanish. Jiménez, as part of this work, also extensively revised and adapted such works as Tagore's *The Crescent Moon*. Indeed, during this time, Jiménez developed the now-heralded innovation of "naked poetry". Ortega y Gasset wrote that "Tagore's wide appeal [may stem from the fact that] he speaks of longings for perfection that we all have ... Tagore awakens a dormant sense of childish wonder, and he saturates the air with all kinds of enchanting promises for the reader, who ... pays little attention to the deeper import of Oriental mysticism". Tagore's works were published in free editions around 1920 alongside works by Dante Alighieri, Miguel de Cervantes, Johann Wolfgang von Goethe, Plato, and Leo Tolstoy. Tagore's talents came to be regarded as overrated by several westerners. Graham Greene doubted that "anyone but Mr. Yeats can still take his poems very seriously." Modern remnants of a once widespread Latin American reverence of Tagore were discovered, for example, by an astonished Salman Rushdie during a trip to Nicaragua.

Life of Rabindranath Tagore (1861–1901)

The life of Rabindranath Tagore (1861–1941) covers the first four decades of his life; these were formative of both his artistic and much of his political thinking. Rabindranath Tagore was a Bengali poet, Brahmo philosopher, and scholar.

Family Background

Tagore was born at No. 6 Dwarkanath Tagore Lane, Jorasanko—the address of his family mansion. In turn, Jorasanko was located in the Bengali section of north Kolkata, located near Chitpur Road. The area immediately around the Jorasanko Tagore mansion was rife with poverty and prostitution. He was the son of Debendranath Tagore and Sarada Devi. Debendranath Tagore had formulated the Brahmo faith propagated by his friend, the reformer Raja Ram Mohan Roy. Debendranath became the central figure in Brahmo society after Ray's death, who was addressed out of respect by followers as *maharishi.* He continued to lead the *Adi Brahmo Samaj* until he died. Women who married into Tagore's clan were generally from the villages of East Bengal (now Bangladesh).

Childhood (1861–1878)

Tagore was born the youngest of fourteen children. As a child, Tagore lived amidst an atmosphere where literary magazines were published, musical recitals were held, and theatre performed. The Jorasanko Tagores were indeed at the center of a large and art-loving social group. Tagore's oldest brother, Dwijendranath, was a respected philosopher and poet. Another brother, Satyendranath, was the first ethnically Indian member appointed to the elite and formerly all-white Indian Civil Service. Yet another brother, Jyotirindranath Tagore, was a talented musician, composer, and playwright. Among his sisters, Swarnakumari Devi earned fame as a novelist in her own right. Jyotirindranath's wife, Kadambari — who was slightly older than Tagore — was a dear friend and a powerful influence on Tagore. Her abrupt suicide in 1884 left him distraught for years, and left a profound mark on the emotional timbre of Tagore's literary life.

Tagore—nicknamed "Rabi"—was born the youngest of fourteen children. As part of the Jorasanko branch of the Tagore family, Tagore grew up exposed to the publication of literary magazines, in-home musical recitals, and theatrical performances. Tagore was also influenced by older brothers Dwijendranath (a philosopher), Satyendranath (the first Indian appointed to the elite Indian Civil Service), and Jyotirindranath (a musician, composer, and playwright). His female relatives included sister Swarna Kumari Devi (a novelist) and Kadambari (Jyotirindranath's wife, whose 1884 suicide burdened Tagore for years).

For the first decade or so of his life, Tagore remained distant from his father, who was frequently away touring northern India, England, and other places. Meanwhile, Tagore was mostly confined to the family compound — he was forbidden to leave it for any purpose other than traveling to school. He thereby grew increasingly restless for the outside world, open spaces, and nature. On the other hand, Tagore was intimidated by the mansion's perceived ghostly and enigmatic aura. Further, Tagore was ordered about the house by servants in a period he would later designate as a "servocracy". Incidents included servants dunking the heads of Tagore and his siblings into drinking water held by giant clay cisterns — used as a means to quiet the children. In addition, Tagore often refused food to satisfy servants, was confined to a chalk circle by the second-in-command servant named Shyam in parody of an analogous forest trial that Sita underwent in the *Ramayana*, and was told horrific stories telling the bloody exploits of outlaw dacoits.

Tagore was also was tutored at home by Hemendranath, his brother. While being physically conditioned — for example, swimming in the Ganges River, taking long treks through hilly areas, and practicing judo and wrestling — he was also given Bengali-language lessons in anatomy, drawing, English language (Tagore's least favourite subject), geography, gymnastics, history, literature, mathematics, and Sanskrit imparted before and after school. Meanwhile, Tagore was developed an aversion towards formal learning and schooling, stating later that the role of teaching was not to explain things, but rather to

> *"knock at the doors of the mind. If any boy is asked to give an account of what is awakened in him by such knocking, he will probably say something silly. For what happens within is much bigger than what comes out in words. Those who pin their faith on university*

examinations as the test of education take no account of this."

Tagore started writing poems around age eight, and he was urged by an older brother to recite these to people in the mansion — including to an impressed Brahmo nationalist, newspaper editor, and Hindu Mela organizer. At age eleven, Tagore underwent the *upanayan* coming-of-age rite: he and two relatives were shaved bald and sent into retreat, where they were to chant and meditate. Tagore instead rollicked, beating drums and pulling his brothers' ears, after which he received a sacred thread of investiture. Afterward, on February 14, 1873, Tagore experienced the first close contact with his father when they set out together from Calcutta on a months-long tour of India. They first made for Shantiniketan ("Abode of Peace"), a family estate acquired in 1863 by Debendranath composed of two rooms set amidst a mango grove, trees, and plants. Tagore later recalled his stay among the rice paddies:

"What I could not see did not take me long to get over — what I did see was quite enough. There was no servant rule, and the only ring which encircled me was the blue of the horizon, drawn around these [rural] solitudes by their presiding goddess. Within this I was free to move about as I chose."

After several weeks, they travelled to Amritsar, staying near the Harmandir Sahib and worshipping at a Sikh gurudwara. They also read English- and Sanskrit-language books, exposing Tagore to astronomy, biographies of such figures as Benjamin Franklin, and Edward Gibbon's *The History of the Decline and Fall of the Roman Empire*. Later, in mid-April, Tagore and his father set off for the remote and frigid Himalayan hill station of Dalhousie, India, near what is now Himachal Pradesh's border with Kashmir.

There, at an elevation of some 2,300 meters (7,500 feet), they lived in a house high atop Bakrota hill. Tagore was taken aback by the region's deep gorges, alpine forests, and mossy streams and waterfalls. Yet Tagore was also made to study lessons—including such things as Sanskrit declensions—starting in the icy pre-dawn twilight. Tagore took a break from his readings for a noontime meal; thereafter, Tagore was to continue his studies, although Tagore was often allowed to fall asleep. Some two months later, Tagore left his father in Dalhousie and journeyed back to Calcutta.

Schooling in England

In early October 1878, Tagore travelled to England with the intent of becoming a barrister. He first stayed for some months at a house that the Tagore family owned near Brighton and Hove, in Medina Villas; there, he attended a Brighton school (not, as has been claimed, Brighton College — his name does not appear in its admissions register). In 1877, his nephew and niece — Suren and Indira, the children of Tagore's brother Satyendranath — were sent together with their mother (Tagore's sister-in-law) to live with him.

Later, after spending Christmas of 1878 with his family, Tagore was escorted by his elder brother's friend to London; there, Tagore's relatives hoped that he would focus more on his studies. He enrolled at University College London. However, he never did complete his degree, leaving England after just over a year's stay. This exposure to English culture and language would later percolate into his earlier acquaintance with Bengali musical tradition, allowing him to create new modes of music, poetry, and drama. Nevertheless, Tagore neither fully embraced English strictures nor his family's traditionally strict Hindu religious observances in either his life or in his art, choosing instead to pick the best from both realms of experience.

Shelaidaha

In 1890, Tagore began managing his family's estates in Shelaidaha, a region now in Bangladesh; he was joined by his wife and children in 1898. Tagore, known then as "Zamindar Babu", often travelled dozens of miles across the vast estate while living out of the *Padma*, the family's converted flat-bottomed keel-less barge (known as a "budgerow" or a *Daccai bajras*). His dealings with his tenants included the annual collection of (mostly token) rents and the blessing of villagers; in exchange for his generosity, villagers regularly held feasts in Tagore's honour — these featured such fare as dried rice and sour milk. In this decade, Tagore authored many works and founded a new genre of Bengali writing: the short story. Tagore wrote some fifty-nine of them in 1891–1901; many had ironic elements or had emotional appeal while they dealt with a wide range of Bengali lifestyles. Examples include *Sonar Tari* (1894), *Chitra* (1896), and *Katha O Kahini* (1900); his essays, poems, and plays of the time also touched on village life.

Life of Rabindranath Tagore (1901–1932)

The life of Rabindranath Tagore (1901–1924) concerns his life in Santiniketan and extensive travels throughout Asia, Europe, and Japan. Rabindranath Tagore was a Bengali poet, Brahmo philosopher, and scholar.

Santiniketan

In 1901, Tagore left Shelaidaha and moved to Shantiniketan, about one hundred miles to Calcutta's northwest in what is now West Bengal. Shantiniketan, a spread of relatively arid and eroded red soil of seven acres bought in the 1860s by Debendranth, was made the home of Tagore's new ashram, a marble-floored prayer hall ("The Mandir"), experimental school, groves of trees, gardens, and a library. Unfortunately, his wife along with two of his children — Renuka (in 1903) and Samindranath (in 1907) — died in this period, leaving Tagore distraught. When Tagore's father — aged 87 — also died on January 19, 1905, Tagore began receiving 1,250–1,500 rupees (Rs.) monthly as an inheritance. This combined with income from the Maharaja of Tripura, sales of jewelry owned by him and his late wife, his bungalow at the seaside Puri, and mediocre royalties (Rs. 2,000) gleaned from the licensed publishing of thousands of copies of his works.

Thus, he gained a large following among Bengali readers. He published such works as *Naivedya* (1901) and *Kheya* (1906). Non-Bangla translations were also published, but these were frequently of mediocre quality. In response to requests by admirers (including painter William Rothenstein), Tagore began translating his poems into free verse. In 1912, he went to

England while carrying a sheaf of his translated works. At readings there, these works impressed a number of Englishmen, including English missionary and Gandhi protege Charles F. Andrews, Anglo-Irish poet William Butler Yeats, Ezra Pound, Robert Bridges, Ernest Rhys, and Thomas Sturge Moore. Indeed, Yeats later wrote the preface to the English translation of Gitanjali (published by the India Society), while Andrews joined Tagore in India to work with him.

On 10 November 1912, Tagore travelled to the United States, speaking at a Unitarian church in Urbana, Illinois. In that year, Tagore also toured the United Kingdom, meeting William Rothenstein and William Butler Yeats, who read his *Gitanjali*. Later, he stayed in Butterton, Staffordshire with C.F. Andrews' clergymen friends. On 14 November 1913, he received word that he had won the Nobel Prize in Literature; the award stemmed from the idealistic and accessible (for Western readers) nature of a small body of translated material, including the 1912 *Gitanjali: Song Offerings*.

Together with Mukul Dey, Charles F. Andrews and W. W. Pearson, Tagore again set off by boat on 3 May 1916, embarking on a lecturing circuit of Japan and the United States that was to last until April 1917. During a four-month layover in Japan, Tagore authored "On the Way to Japan" and "In Japan", which were later compiled into the book *Japanyatri* ("A Sojourn to Japan"), which detailed his admiration for the Japanese aesthetic. Yet Tagore also denounced nationalism, particularly that of the Japanese and Americans. He wrote the essay "Nationalism in India", attracting both derision and praise (the latter from pacifists and fellow internationalists like Romain Rolland). Yet these views also endangered him: during his stay in a San Francisco hotel, Tagore narrowly escaped being assassinated by a pair of Indian expatriates — the plot failed only because the would-be assassins fell into argument concerning whether they should carry through with the murder. The following morning, Tagore left for Santa Barbara, near Los Angeles. There, Tagore meditated among orange groves and conceived of a new type of university, desiring to "make Shantiniketan the connecting thread between India and the world ... [and] a world center for the study of humanity ... somewhere beyond the limits of nation and geography."

The school — which he named Visva-Bharati — had its foundation stone ceremoniously laid on 22 December 1918; it was later inaugurated on 22 December 1921. Tagore's duties as steward and mentor at Santiniketan kept him busy; he taught classes in mornings and wrote textbooks for his students in afternoons and evenings. Of this routine, he wrote that "I long to discover some fairyland of holidays ... where all duties look delightfully undutiful, like clouds bearing rain appearing perfectly inconsequential". Tagore was also occupied with fundraising between 1919 and 1921, undertaking trips to Europe and the U.S.

Life of Rabindranath Tagore (1932–1941)

Last Works of 1932-1937

Tagore's international travels also sharpened his opinion that human divisions were shallow. During a May 1932 visit to a Bedouin encampment in the Iraqi desert, the tribal chief told him that "Our prophet has said that a true Muslim is he by whose words and deeds not the least of his brother-men may ever come to any harm ..." Tagore noted in his diary: "I was startled into recognizing in his words the voice of essential humanity."

In his last decade, Tagore compiled fifteen volumes of writings, including works of prose-poems such as *Punashcha* (1932), *Shes Saptak* (1935), and *Patraput* (1936). He also continued his experimentations by developing prose-songs and dance-dramas, including *Chitrangada* (1936), *Shyama* (1939), and *Chandalika* (1938). He also wrote the novels *Dui Bon* (1933), *Malancha* (1934), and *Char Adhyay* (1934). Tagore also took an interest in science in his last years, writing *Visva-Parichay* (a collection of essays) in 1937. He wrote on topics ranging from biology to physics, and astronomy; meanwhile, his poetry — containing extensive naturalism — underscored his respect for scientific laws. He also wove the process of science (including narratives of scientists) into many stories contained in such volumes as *Se* (1937), *Tin Sangi* (1940), and *Galpasalpa* (1941).

Illness of 1937-1941

Tagore's last four years (1937–1941) were marked by chronic pain and two long periods of illness. These began when Tagore lost consciousness in late 1937; he remained comatose and near death for an extended period. This was followed three years later in late 1940 by a similar spell, from which he never recovered. The poetry Tagore wrote in these twilight years are distinctive for their preoccupation with death; these more profound and mystical experimentations allowed Tagore to be branded a "modern poet". After extended suffering, Tagore died on August 7, 1941 (22 Shravan 1348) in an upstairs room of the Jorasanko mansion in which he was raised. This date is still mourned in public functions held across the Bangla-speaking world.

The last person to see Tagore alive was Amiya Kumar Sen (brother of Sukumar Sen, the first chief election commissioner); Tagore dictated his last poem to Sen, who wrote it down. Sen later donated the resulting draft to a museum in Kolkata.

Chokher Bali

Chokher Bali, literally *Sand of the Eye*, equivalent to *eye-sore*, is a Bengali novel written by Rabindranath Tagore in the early twentieth century, against the backdrop of the Indian Independence Movement.

Plot Summary

Binodini is a young widow left to her own devices when her sickly husband dies soon after they are married. She returns to her village and lives there for a couple of months until she accepts the invitation of Rajlakshmi to live with her and her son, Mahendra (who had rejected a former marriage proposal with Binodini). He is newly married to Ashalata, but eventually realises that he and Binodini are more compatible. The story details the relationships of these three and Mahendra's best friend Behari as they deal with issues like distrust, adultery, lies, and numerous fallings-out between them.

Critical Acclaim

Tagore elaborately records early 20th century Bengali society, through his central character, the rebellious widow, who wants to live a life of her own. In writing this novel he exposes the custom of perpetual mourning on the part of widows, who were not allowed to remarry and were condemned to a life of seclusion and loneliness. It is a melancholy, stirring tale of the deceit and sorrow that arise from dissatisfaction and sorrow. Tagore has said about the novel, "I have always regretted the ending".

Adaptations

Gitanjali

Gitanjali (Bangla *Gitanjoli*) is a collection of 103 English poems, largely translations, by the Bengali poet Rabindranath Tagore. This volume became very famous in the West, and was widely translated. Gitanjali is also the title of an earlier Bengali volume (1910) of mostly devotional songs. The word *gitanjoli* is a composed from "git", song, and "anjoli", offering, and thus means - "An offering of songs"; but the word for offering, *anjoli*, has a strong devotional connotation, so the title may also be interpreted as "prayer offering of song".

The English collection is not a translation of poems from the Bengali volume of the same name. While half the poems (52 out of 103) in the English text were selected from the Bengali volume, others were taken from these works (given with year and number of songs selected for the English text): *Gitimallo* (1914,17), *Noibeddo* (1901,15), *Khea* (1906,11) and a handful from other works. The translations were often radical, leaving out or altering large chunks of the poem and in one instance even fusing two separate poems (song 95, which unifies songs 89,90 of naivedya).

The translations were undertaken prior to a visit to England in 1912, where the poems were extremely well received. A slender volume was published in 1913, with an exhilarating preface by W. B. Yeats. In the same year, based on a corpus of three thin translations, Rabindranath became the first non-European to win the Nobel prize.

Poetry

The poems of Gitanjali express a largely metaphysical outlook, talking about a union with the "supreme"; but like much western poetry that explores similar themes, the language suggests the union of two earthly lovers. This type of anthropomorphic depiction of celestial love is quite common in the Vaishnava literature of India since the 12th c.. Rabindranath encountered it also in his interactions with the Baul community in rural Bengal. For example, poem 7 in the English volume renders poem 125 from the Bengali Gitanjali, *Amar e gan chheechhe tar shôkol ôlongkar* and talks of heavenly love in terms of the lover taking off her jewelry, which is getting in the way of the union. See also the poem 18, at the bottom of this page.

Some poems involve themes related to nature, but here, too, the spiritual is subtly present, as in this poem (no. 57), given here along with the Bangla text in Roman script:

Light, my light, the world-filling light, the eye-kissing light, heart-sweetening light!

Ah, the light dances, my darling, at the centre of my life; the light strikes, my darling, the chords of my love; the sky opens, the wind runs wild, laughter passes over the earth.

The butterflies spread their sails on the sea of light. Lilies and jasmines surge up on the crest of the waves of light.

The light is shattered into gold on every cloud, my darling, and it scatters gems in profusion.

Mirth spreads from leaf to leaf, my darling, and gladness without measure. The heaven's river has drowned its banks and the flood of joy is abroad.

Alo amar, alo ogo, alo bhubôn bhôraalo nôeon dhôoa amar, alo hridôe hara.Nache alo nache, o bhai, amar praner kachhe

—baje alo baje, o bhai, hridôe binar majhe—jage akash, chhoþe batash, hashe shôkol dhôra. Alor srote pal tulechhe hajar projapoti. Alor ðheue uþhlo mete mollika maloti. Meghe meghe shona, o bhai, jae na manik gona—patae patae hashi, o bhai, pulôk rashi rashi. Shuronodir kul bhorechhe shudha-nijhôr-jhôra. -Ôcholaeotôn

Writing on the Screen: Satyajit Ray's Adaptation of Tagore

I

As we think of the models of adaptation we are forced to work with formal definitions of literature or film. It is necessary to recognise the modes and limits of transaction, and that demands positing stable entities between which the transaction takes place. Nevertheless, we also know that it is not a medium but a practice that one has to think of as literary or film texts are produced, practice being itself always adaptive, always redefining the borders between what falls within the medium and what does not. To place adaptation in a historical context could mean considering practice itself as something that conditions the medium rather than the other way round. Besides social and historical contexts one has to also consider here the contexts of the media in question, their own levels of historical development. I would like to illustrate the point with the help of a modern classic from India, Satyajit Ray's *Charulata* (1964).

Soon after the release of *Charulata*, Ray became involved in an intense debate over the changes he made in the original text, 'Nastaneer' ('The Broken Nest'), a 1901 story written by Rabindranath Tagore (Ray 1982). An eminent critic called into question the very necessity of presenting the film as an adaptation of Tagore, whatever the merits of the film were, after such changes as those that Ray brought into 'both the theme and the plot' of the film (Rudra 1996). The story has the structure of a novelette; it is divided into twenty short chapters posing a challenge to a filmmaker who is looking for a tightly integrated narrative. The critic pointed out how Ray has virtually done away with the material of the last seven chapters and added several new elements, to mark a definite break with Tagore. Can departure itself be a mode of adaptation? Ray's reply came up with the most extensive analysis he ever wrote of his own films. He defended the deviations from the original in terms of the treatment of time, causality and character delineation, and in the process explained the primary imperatives of storytelling in cinema.

The story is set in the late nineteenth century Bengal. Bhupati, a well-meaning member of the nationalist gentry, spends most of his time on the political magazine he brings out in English. His young wife Charulata, following the custom, is confined to the inner quarters of the house, spends lonely hours reading novels and doing embroidery. She finds a companion in Bhupati's cousin Amal, a university student of her age. They exchange knowledge of novels, share enthusiasm for literary periodicals, they help each other grow into creative writers. All this happens with encouragement from Bhupati. For Amal, the realisation will come too late that the relationship has grown into love; and he will be in a position to break away from the bond, he will leave the house. For Charu, this organic aspect of growing up, of articulating herself into the world, will not be as easy to disown. She creates a new secret interior within the interior she inhabits as she learns to live with the new reality. Bhupati will come to know about all this after Charu has built that secret chamber, after she returns to him as a wife, so to speak. This discovery of the truth of the home also comes for Bhupati after his public enterprise, the magazine, fails, when he comes back to the inner quarters seeking his wife's company for the first time (see Tagore 1992).

In his essay, Ray explains the basic rules of screenwriting and direction in order to point out the specificity of his medium. The debate took place in the pages of one of the most prestigious literary periodicals of the time, *Parichay*, the readers and contributors of which might have been intellectually advanced in other ways but seemed to require a lesson in film language. The film society movement was still in its early phase, and it is Ray the film society activist speaking here, still engaged in some kind of awareness raising exercise, making audiences familiar with arguments about the autonomy of film. The struggle for autonomy is launched here against a 'literary' perception of cinema.

Ray was one of the founders of the Calcutta Film Society, the first of its kind in India, established in 1947. The critical discourse that he and his colleagues at the Film Society launched can be seen in many ways as a preamble to the realist break that Ray's debut film, *Pather Panchali*, brought about in 1955. But serious discussion of cinema began before this cineaste intervention, it goes back at least to the late 1920s. A spate of film magazines followed the arrival of sound in 1931. The new sound studios employed a large number of writers. Sound redefined Indian cinema in terms of regional practices, regions being linguistically divided in India. A language - cinema-literature correspondence was established in critical discourse which also set into relief the categories of realism, authenticity and authorship. Writings on cinema from the 1930s and 40s, often by the writers and critics who had joined the industry, present a more or less consistent argument for a regionally grounded contemporary cinema that should mould itself into a novelistic discourse. The *Mythological* film, often thought to be characteristic of Indian popular cinema, became a minor genre in the sound cinema of the Studio Era (1931-55), giving way to the *Social* film as the dominant mode. The *Social* was the mainstream middle-class cinema negotiating the theme of social reform that has informed the novel in all Indian languages since the nineteenth century. The mutations set in motion in the *Social* in the 1940s will finally give rise to two formations, the realist art film launched with *Pather Panchali*, and the classic melodrama that came into being around the same time that *Pather Panchali* appeared.

The question of autonomy figured prominently in the new criticism that arrived in the wake of the Calcutta Film Society. Informed by an exposure to world cinema this criticism came to posit the idea of a national modern cinema, a cinema that would fashion a rational, democratic language free of the pre-modern, non-secular compulsions of the popular film. The arguments for textual autonomy and for rational form were of necessity interrelated. The heteronomous address of Indian popular cinema, where blocks of spectacle are often combined through a logic of interruption, was the target of this critical discourse; but initially, there was also an older practice of the Studio- *Social* that had to be confronted. This was a kind of 'cinema du papa' - dominated by literary practitioners, where screenplays and films were often judged on the basis of the literary value of dialogue and characters. Major novelists such as Premendra Mitra and Sailajananda Mukhopadhyay were seen to have failed to break into a cinematic language because of their inability to conceive such language in its autonomy. Ray's defence of his adaptation is pitched against the lingering resistance to perceiving the film text in its own terms, the challenge being all the more serious here because of the Tagore factor.

II

Can we judge *Charulata* on the basis of its independence of literary procedures, of the generic protocols of the original story? As we watch the film adaptation itself becomes an object of scrutiny. We relish the transformation that Tagore's rich prose has undergone in the wordless passages of *Charulata*, enjoy the method that translates spaces between the words into volume and movement. But there is a second level of contact between the two texts where the whole question of word and image transaction has to be re-considered. At this level, the film takes its distance in time from the original text as a material basis of adaptation; it begins to look at a past of which the literary text itself has become a constitutive element. Hence it was not only the camera penetrating the world captured in the story in order to transform it into another language, it was also a question of framing the story itself as part of a fabric of the past.

'Broken Nest' reads more like a compressed novel than a short story, it moves through extended passages and gaps in time, through episodes and broad developments in characters and situations. The long introductory sequence of *Charulata* is probably the best example of the masterly technique of compression and telescoping Ray uses to translate descriptive passages. Almost without any dialogue the sequence establishes a typical afternoon in Charu's life, her loneliness, her affinity to novels, the spatial limits of her movements. It brings to life an object-world that embodies time – the wallpaper, the furniture, the items of daily use, but also the street sounds and the street images. These images are glimpsed by Charu through an opera glass: as she opens one blind after another on the wall to peek at the comically graphic characters moving in the street, her socially restricted movement momentarily turns into a playful choreography. And then Charu frames the figure of her husband Bhupati with the opera glass - passing down the corridor not noticing her, lost in his book. Ray conjures up this interior with a dexterity that reminds us of the image of Charu's embroidery in the title sequence, A texture of words is dissolved into a weave of images effortlessly before our eyes.

But the world that is conjured up is also a world of texts in *Charulata.* And at this level, the cinematic moves are negotiated through literature rather than in terms of separation from it. The alphabet that Charu embroiders on the handkerchief signals the insistence of the letter in the film. The written word will take on a particular luminosity as the film progresses, and the world of writing that is invoked in the opening sequence will form the very basis of the re-created time and place. Charu hums the name of her favourite novelist, Bankim, as she browses idly through the bookshelf. Bankimchandra Chatterjee was a pioneer of the novel form in India and a crucial ideologue of nationalism. The film constantly refers to his novels; through a shared knowledge of these novels Charu and Amal come close to each other. Bhupati, and Charu's sister-in-law, Manda, fall outside this domain of exchange because of their lack of appreciation of Bankim. The name of Bankim will end up in a play of alliteration between Charu and Amal in their last extended conversation.

At a more discursive level, the whole film can be seen to be engaged in a dialogue with one of Bankim's essays, 'Women, Old and New', a major statement on what is known as the 'Women's Question' in the nineteenth century. All this is added to Tagore's original text which finds itself embedded in a tapestry of literary signs. Writers people the world - Taraknath Gangopadhyay, Rammohun Roy, Shakespeare, Byron, Addison, Steele, Emerson.

The image of writing, the written word, forms a major visual motif – we closely watch Amal writing, Charu writing, Bhupati getting intoxicated with the printed word. The alphabet shining on the embroidery over the titles signals a process which will lead us to the very last image of the film: the hands of Charu and Bhupati freeze before they could meet, the title of Tagore's story appears on the screen in calligraphic design. This would appear as merely explanatory and redundant (to say 'Broken Nest' here is to be literal) unless we follow the logic of appearance of the written word in the film. It is a final gesture of receding from the original story, of turning the work itself into an object of the film's gaze. The scene in which Bhupati comes to know about Charu's feelings for his cousin the camera makes a gesture very unusual for Ray: it climbs up the leg of a marble table slowly to reveal a letter lying on it while Charu and Bhupati are heard talking off-screen. The letter is from Amal and it will bring about an emotional outburst in Charu giving her feelings away. The very tendentious movement of the camera, drawing attention to the letter as the dramatic agent, would look odd in a work of concealed narration unless one remembers the role of the letter as such in the film.

Bankim's 'Women Old and New' was published in 1879 (Ray gives an exact time for the events, 1879, as we know from the dateline on the copy of the magazine that Bhupati shows Amal) where he argues for a new woman who would be modern in the traditional way. She would embody the resolution of the conflict between tradition and modernity by finding her place in a re-invented patriarchy. She would learn to be the new old woman. As the film launches a dialogue with this essay it maps Tagore's story onto a historical grid, the political drama is brought out into the open. The story tells us of the formation of the colonial subject, male and female, and of the inevitable irony and pain that attend the process. Tagore begins his story by an ironic description of the domains his characters occupy.

The idealistic, English educated Bhupati is worried about the expansion of British territories beyond the Afghan borders, but hasn't had the time to notice how his child bride has bloomed into womanhood; Charu's idleness is of a different kind, reminding one of a fruitless tree. As she develops an expressive selfhood, through her love and through her writing, the challenge of the demarcation of domains comes to face her, it demands a heavy price. Tagore, writing more or less from within the social reality that he portrays, was not in a position to uncover the historical dynamics of this matrix. Ray casts a historical gaze at the story at this level too; he creates a design with characters and spaces and distributes the story along discursive lines of divide. The dichotomy of literature and politics suggested in the story is developed into a strong motif in the film. The first is associated with the woman, the second belongs to the man. Bhupati entrusts Amal with Charu's literary education admitting that he has no taste for such things, busy as he is with the 'real world' of politics. Ray also makes him say to Amal that this politics, critical though it is of the colonial government's policies, is not meant to be disloyal to the masters. And from Bhupati we also learn that how worried he and friends are about the outcome of the parliamentary elections in Britain; one of his friends has vowed to sacrifice a goat at the Kali temple if the liberals win.

Bhupati writes politics in English, Amal and Charu write literature in Bengali. And then we come to a further division: Amal writes for public circulation, in an ornate register, Charu would like to write for a strictly private exchange, in an unadorned style through which she can evoke personal experiences. Towards the end, after Amal has left the house and Bhupati's magazine has failed, Charu and Bhupati go on a visit to the seaside and plan a poignantly illusory reconciliation between the poles of opposition – between the public and the private, home and the world, politics and culture. Why not bring out another magazine, they propose, which will have politics in English and literature in Bengali.

One can see Charu never believing in this. She is coming to a harder knowledge, she has had to grow up paying a dreadful price. The film brings out this irony of growing up in its most acute historical-political dimensions. It does away with a whole lot of events present in the original story not so much to bring out its essence but the political essence of the predicament that it deals with. Growing into modernity, into citizenship, into subjectivity of a nameable kind - all this, marked indelibly with the reality of living through colonialism, would not have been so strongly captured without the grand design of polarities that the film is grounded in. In devising his language Ray moves in and out of the field of literature, it would be difficult to recognise this aspect of his craft if we conceived of literature or film in their pure autonomy.

●●●

2

Tagore and His India

Voice of Bengal

Rabindranath Tagore, who died in 1941 at the age of eighty, is a towering figure in the millennium-old literature of Bengal. Anyone who becomes familiar with this large and flourishing tradition will be impressed by the power of Tagore's presence in Bangladesh and in India. His poetry as well as his novels, short stories, and essays are very widely read, and the songs he composed reverberate around the eastern part of India and throughout Bangladesh.

In contrast, in the rest of the world, especially in Europe and America, the excitement that Tagore's writings created in the early years of the twentieth century has largely vanished. The enthusiasm with which his work was once greeted was quite remarkable. *Gitanjali,* a selection of his poetry for which he was awarded the Nobel Prize in Literature in 1913, was published in English translation in London in March of that year, and had been reprinted ten times by November, when the award was announced. But he is not much read now in the West, and already by 1937, Graham Greene was able to say: "As for Rabindranath Tagore, I cannot believe that anyone but Mr. Yeats can still take his poems very seriously."

The Mystic

The contrast between Tagore's commanding presence in Bengali literature and culture, and his near-total eclipse in the rest of the world, is perhaps less interesting than the distinction between the view of Tagore as a deeply relevant and manysided contemporary thinker in Bangladesh and India, and his image in the West as a repetitive and remote spiritualist. Graham Greene had, in fact, gone on to explain that he associated Tagore "with what Chesterton calls 'the bright pebbly eyes' of the Theosophists." Certainly, an air of mysticism played some part in the "selling" of Rabindranath Tagore to the West by Yeats, Ezra Pound, and his other early champions. Even Anna Akhmatova, one of Tagore's few later admirers (who translated his poems into Russian in the mid-1960s), talks of "that mighty flow of poetry which takes its strength from Hinduism as from the Ganges, and is called Rabindranath Tagore."

Confluence of Cultures

Rabindranath did come from a Hindu family—one of the landed gentry who owned estates mostly in what is now Bangladesh. But whatever wisdom there might be in Akhmatova's invoking of Hinduism and the Ganges, it did not prevent the largely Muslim citizens of Bangladesh from having a deep sense of identity with Tagore and his ideas. Nor did it stop the newly independent Bangladesh from choosing one of Tagore's songs—the "Amar Sonar Bangla" which means "my golden Bengal"—as its national anthem. This must be very confusing to those who see the contemporary world as a "clash of civilizations"—with "the Muslim civilization," "the Hindu civilization," and "the Western civilization," each forcefully confronting the others. They would also be confused by Rabindranath Tagore's own description of his Bengali family as the product of "a confluence of three cultures: Hindu, Mohammedan, and British".

Rabindranath's grandfather, Dwarkanath, was well known for his command of Arabic and Persian, and Rabindranath grew up in a family atmosphere in which a deep knowledge of Sanskrit and ancient Hindu texts was combined with an understanding of Islamic traditions as well as Persian literature. It is not so much that Rabindranath tried to produce—or had an interest in producing—a "synthesis" of the different religions (as the great Mughal emperor Akbar tried hard to achieve) as that his outlook was persistently non-sectarian, and his writings—some two hundred books—show the influence of different parts of the Indian cultural background as well as of the rest of the world.

Abode of Peace

Most of his work was written at Santiniketan (Abode of Peace), the small town that grew around the school he founded in Bengal in 1901, and he not only conceived there an imaginative and innovative system of education, but through his writings and his influence on students and teachers, he was able to use the school as a base from which he could take a major part in India's social, political, and cultural movements.

The profoundly original writer, whose elegant prose and magical poetry Bengali readers know well, is not the sermonizing spiritual guru admired—and then rejected—in London. Tagore was not only an immensely versatile poet; he was also a great short story writer, novelist, playwright, essayist, and composer of songs, as well as a talented painter whose pictures, with their mixture of representation and abstraction, are only now beginning to receive the acclaim that they have long deserved. His essays, moreover, ranged over literature, politics, culture, social change, religious beliefs, philosophical analysis, international relations, and much else. The coincidence of the fiftieth anniversary of Indian independence with the publication of a selection of Tagore's letters by Cambridge University Press , brought Tagore's ideas and reflections to the fore, which makes it important to examine what kind of leadership in thought and understanding he provided in the Indian subcontinent in the first half of this century.

Gandhi and Tagore

Since Rabindranath Tagore and Mohandas Gandhi were two leading Indian thinkers in the twentieth century, many commentators have tried to compare their ideas. On learning of Rabindranath's death, Jawaharlal Nehru, then incarcerated in a British jail in India, wrote in his prison diary for August 7, 1941:

"Gandhi and Tagore. Two types entirely different from each other, and yet both of them typical of India, both in the long line of India's great men ... It is not so much because of any single virtue but because of the tout ensemble, *that I felt that among the world's great men today Gandhi and Tagore were supreme as human beings. What good fortune for me to have come into close contact with them."*

Romain Rolland was fascinated by the contrast between them, and when he completed his book on Gandhi, he wrote to an Indian academic, in March 1923: "I have finished my *Gandhi,* in which I pay tribute to your two great river-like souls, overflowing with divine spirit, Tagore and Gandhi." The following month, he recorded in his diary an account of some of the differences between Gandhi and Tagore written by Reverend C.F. Andrews, the English clergyman and public activist who was a close friend of both men (and whose important role in Gandhi's life in South Africa as well as India is well portrayed in Richard Attenborough's film Gandhi [1982]). Andrews described to Rolland a discussion between Tagore and Gandhi, at which he was present, on subjects that divided them:

"The first subject of discussion was idols; Gandhi defended them, believing the masses incapable of raising themselves immediately to abstract ideas. Tagore cannot bear to see the people eternally treated as a child. Gandhi quoted the great things achieved in Europe by the flag as an idol; Tagore found it easy to object, but Gandhi held his ground, contrasting European flags bearing eagles, etc., with his own, on which he has put a spinning wheel. The second point of discussion was nationalism, which Gandhi defended. He said that one must go through nationalism to reach internationalism, in the same way that one must go through war to reach peace."

Tagore greatly admired Gandhi but he had many disagreements with him on a variety of subjects, including nationalism, patriotism, the importance of cultural exchange, the role of rationality and of science, and the nature of economic and social development. These differences, I shall argue, have a clear and consistent pattern, with Tagore pressing for more room for reasoning, and for a less traditionalist view, a greater interest in the rest of the world, and more respect for science and for objectivity generally.

Rabindranath knew that he could not have given India the political leadership that Gandhi provided, and he was never stingy in his praise for what Gandhi did for the nation (it was, in fact, Tagore who popularized the term "Mahatma"—great soul—as a description of Gandhi). And yet each remained deeply critical of many things that the other stood for. That Mahatma Gandhi has received incomparably more attention outside India and also within much of India itself makes it important to understand "Tagore's side" of the Gandhi-Tagore debates.

In his prison diary, Nehru wrote: "Perhaps it is as well that [Tagore] died now and did not see the many horrors that are likely to descend in increasing measure on the world and on India. He had seen enough and he was infinitely sad and unhappy." Toward the end of his life, Tagore was indeed becoming discouraged about the state of India, especially as its normal burden of problems, such as hunger and poverty, was being supplemented by politically organized incitement to "communal" violence between Hindus and Muslims. This conflict would lead in 1947, six years after Tagore's death, to the widespread killing that took place during partition; but there was much gore already during his declining days. In December 1939, he wrote to his friend Leonard Elmhirst, the English philanthropist and social reformer who had worked closely with him on rural reconstruction in India (and who had gone on to found the Dartington Hall Trust in England and a progressive school at Dartington that explicitly invoked Rabindranath's educational ideals):

> *"It does not need a defeatist to feel deeply anxious about the future of millions who, with all their innate culture and their peaceful traditions are being simultaneously subjected to hunger, disease, exploitations foreign and indigenous, and the seething discontents of communalism."*

How would Tagore have viewed the India of today? Would he see progress there, or wasted opportunity, perhaps even a betrayal of its promise and conviction? And, on a wider subject, how would he react to the spread of cultural separatism in the contemporary world?

East and West

Given the vast range of his creative achievements, perhaps the most astonishing aspect of the image of Tagore in the West is its narrowness; he is recurrently viewed as "the great mystic from the East," an image with a putative message for the West, which some would welcome, others dislike, and still others find deeply boring. To a great extent this Tagore was the West's own creation, part of its tradition of message-seeking from the East, particularly from India, which—as Hegel put it—had "existed for millennia in the imagination of the Europeans." Friedrich Schlegel, Schelling, Herder, and Schopenhauer were only a few of the thinkers who followed the same pattern.

They theorized, at first, that India was the source of superior wisdom. Schopenhauer at one stage even argued that the New Testament "must somehow be of Indian origin: this is attested by its completely Indian ethics, which transforms morals into asceticism, its pessimism, and its avatar," in "the person of Christ." But then they rejected their own theories with great vehemence, sometimes blaming India for not living up to their unfounded expectations.

We can imagine that Rabindranath's physical appearance—handsome, bearded, dressed in non-Western clothes—may, to some extent, have encouraged his being seen as a carrier of exotic wisdom. Yasunari Kawabata, the first Japanese Nobel Laureate in Literature, treasured memories from his middle-school days of "this sage-like poet":

His white hair flowed softly down both sides of his forehead; the tufts of hair under the temples also were long like two beards, and linking up with the hair on his cheeks, continued into his beard, so that he gave an impression, to the boy I was then, of some ancient Oriental wizard.

That appearance would have been well-suited to the selling of Tagore in the West as a quintessentially mystical poet, and it could have made it somewhat easier to pigeonhole him. Commenting on Rabindranath's appearance, Frances Cornford told William Rothenstein, "I can now imagine a powerful and gentle Christ, which I never could before." Beatrice Webb, who did not like Tagore and resented what she took to be his "quite obvious dislike of all that the Webbs stand for" (there is, in fact, little evidence that Tagore had given much thought to this subject), said that he was "beautiful to look at" and that "his speech has the perfect intonation and slow chant-like moderation of the dramatic saint." Ezra Pound and W. B. Yeats, among others, first led the chorus of adoration in the Western appreciation of Tagore, and then soon moved to neglect and even shrill criticism.

The contrast between Yeats's praise of his work in 1912 ("These lyrics...display in their thought a world I have dreamed of all my life long," "the work of a supreme culture") and his denunciation in 1935 ("Damn Tagore") arose partly from the inability of Tagore's manysided writings to fit into the narrow box in which Yeats wanted to place—and keep—him. Certainly, Tagore did write a huge amount, and published ceaselessly, even in English (sometimes in indifferent English translation), but Yeats was also bothered, it is clear, by the difficulty of fitting Tagore's later writings into the image Yeats had presented to the West. Tagore, he had said, was the product of "a whole people, a whole civilization, immeasurably strange to us," and yet "we have met our own image,...or heard, perhaps for the first time in literature, our voice as in a dream."

Yeats did not totally reject his early admiration (as Ezra Pound and several others did), and he included some of Tagore's early poems in *The Oxford Book of Modern Verse,* which he edited in 1936. Yeats also had some favourable things to say about Tagore's prose writings. His censure of Tagore's later poems was reinforced by his dislike of Tagore's own English translations of his work ("Tagore does not know English, no Indian knows English," Yeats explained), unlike the English version of *Gitanjali* which Yeats had himself helped to prepare.

Poetry is, of course, notoriously difficult to translate, and anyone who knows Tagore's poems in their original Bengali cannot feel satisfied with any of the translations (made with or without Yeats's help). Even the translations of his prose works suffer, to some extent, from distortion. E.M. Forster noted, in a review of a translation of one of Tagore's great Bengali novels, *The Home and the World,* in 1919: "The theme is so beautiful," but the charms have "vanished in translation," or perhaps "in an experiment that has not quite come off."

Tagore himself played a somewhat bemused part in the boom and bust of his English reputation. He accepted the extravagant praise with much surprise as well as pleasure, and then received denunciations with even greater surprise, and barely concealed pain. Tagore was sensitive to criticism, and was hurt by even the most far-fetched accusations, such as the charge that he was getting credit for the work of Yeats, who had "rewritten" Gitanjali. (This charge was made by a correspondent for The Times, Sir Valentine Chirol, whom E.M. Forster once described as "an old Anglo-Indian reactionary hack.") From time to time Tagore also protested the crudity of some of his overexcited advocates. He wrote to C.F. Andrews in 1920: "These people...are like drunkards who are afraid of their lucid intervals."

God and Others

Yeats was not wrong to see a large religious element in Tagore's writings. He certainly had interesting and arresting things to say about life and death. Susan Owen, the mother of Wilfred Owen, wrote to Rabindranath in 1920, describing her last conversations with her son before he left for the war which would take his life. Wilfred said goodbye with "those wonderful words of yours—beginning at 'When I go from hence, let this be my parting word.'" When Wilfred's pocket notebook was returned to his mother, she found "these words written in his dear writing—with your name beneath."

The idea of a direct, joyful, and totally fearless relationship with God can be found in many of Tagore's religious writings, including the poems of *Gitanjali.* From India's diverse religious traditions he drew many ideas, both from ancient texts and from popular poetry. But "the bright pebbly eyes of the Theosophists" do not stare out of his verses. Despite the archaic language of the original translation of *Gitanjali,* which did not, I believe, help to preserve the simplicity of the original, its elementary humanity comes through more clearly than any complex and intense spirituality:

Leave this chanting and singing and telling of beads! Whom dost thou worship in this lonely dark corner of a temple with doors all shut?

Open thine eyes and see thy God is not before thee!

He is there where the tiller is tilling the hard ground and where the pathmaker is breaking stones.

He is with them in sun and in shower, and his garment is covered with dust.

An ambiguity about religious experience is central to many of Tagore's devotional poems, and makes them appeal to readers irrespective of their beliefs; but excessively detailed interpretation can ruinously strip away that ambiguity. This applies particularly to his many poems which combine images of human love and those of pious devotion. Tagore writes:

I have no sleep to-night. Ever and again I open my door and look out on the darkness, my friend!

I can see nothing before me. I wonder where lies thy path!

By what dim shore of the ink-black river, by what far edge of the frowning forest, through what mazy depth of gloom, art thou threading thy course to come to see me, my friend?

I suppose it could be helpful to be told, as Yeats hastens to explain, that "the servant or the bride awaiting the master's home-coming in the empty house" is "among the images of the heart turning to God." But in Yeats's considerate attempt to make sure that the reader does not miss the "main point," something of the enigmatic beauty of the Bengali poem is lost - even what had survived the antiquated language of the English translation. Tagore certainly had strongly held religious beliefs (of an unusually nondenominational kind), but he was interested in a great many other things as well and had many different things to say about them.

Some of the ideas he tried to present were directly political, and they figure rather prominently in his letters and lectures. He had practical, plainly expressed views about nationalism, war and peace, cross-cultural education, freedom of the mind, the importance of rational criticism, the need for openness, and so on. His admirers in the West, however, were tuned to the more otherworldly themes which had been emphasized by his first Western patrons. People came to his public lectures in Europe and America, expecting ruminations on grand, transcendental themes; when they heard instead his views on the way public leaders should behave, there was some resentment, particularly (as E.P. Thompson reports) when he delivered political criticism "at $700 a scold."

Reasoning in Freedom

For Tagore it was of the highest importance that people be able to live, and reason, in freedom. His attitudes toward politics and culture, nationalism and internationalism, tradition and modernity, can all be seen in the light of this belief. Nothing, perhaps, expresses his values as clearly as a poem in *Gitanjali:*

> *Where the mind is without fear and the head is held high;*
>
> *Where knowledge is free;*
>
> *Where the world has not been broken up into fragments by narrow domestic walls; ...*
>
> *Where the clear stream of reason has not lost its way into the dreary desert sand of dead habit; ...*
>
> *Into that heaven of freedom, my Father, let my country awake.*

Rabindranath's qualified support for nationalist movements—and his opposition to the unfreedom of alien rule—came from this commitment. So did his reservations about patriotism, which, he argued, can limit both the freedom to engage ideas from outside "narrow domestic walls" and the freedom also to support the causes of people in other countries.

Rabindranath's passion for freedom underlies his firm opposition to unreasoned traditionalism, which makes one a prisoner of the past (lost, as he put it, in "the dreary desert sand of dead habit").

Tagore illustrates the tyranny of the past in his amusing yet deeply serious parable "Kartar Bhoot" ("The Ghost of the Leader"). As the respected leader of an imaginary land is about to die, his panic-stricken followers request him to stay on after his death to instruct them on what to do. He consents. But his followers find their lives are full of rituals and constraints on everyday behaviour and are not responsive to the world around them. Ultimately, they request the ghost of the leader to relieve them of his domination, when he informs them that he exists only in their minds.

Tagore's deep aversion to any commitment to the past that could not be modified by contemporary reason extended even to the alleged virtue of invariably keeping past promises. On one occasion when Mahatma Gandhi visited Tagore's school at Santiniketan, a young woman got him to sign her autograph book. Gandhi wrote: "Never make a promise in haste. Having once made it fulfil it at the cost of your life." When he saw this entry, Tagore became agitated. He wrote in the same book a short poem in Bengali to the effect that no one can be made "a prisoner forever with a chain of clay." He went on to conclude in English, possibly so that Gandhi could read it too, "Fling away your promise if it is found to be wrong."

Tagore had the greatest admiration for Mahatma Gandhi as a person and as a political leader, but he was also highly skeptical of Gandhi's form of nationalism and his conservative instincts regarding the country's past traditions. He never criticized Gandhi personally. In the 1938 essay, "Gandhi the Man," he wrote:

Great as he is as a politician, as an organizer, as a leader of men, as a moral reformer, he is greater than all these as a man, because none of these aspects and activities limits his humanity. They are rather inspired and sustained by it.

And yet there is a deep division between the two men. Tagore was explicit about his disagreement:

> *We who often glorify our tendency to ignore reason, installing in its place blind faith, valuing it as spiritual, are ever paying for its cost with the obscuration of our mind and destiny. I blamed Mahatmaji for exploiting this irrational force of credulity in our people, which might have had a quick result [in creating] a superstructure, while sapping the foundation. Thus began my estimate of Mahatmaji, as the guide of our nation, and it is fortunate for me that it did not end there.*

But while it "did not end there," that difference of vision was a powerful divider. Tagore, for example, remained unconvinced of the merit of Gandhi's forceful advocacy that everyone should spin at home with the "charka," the primitive spinning wheel. For Gandhi this practice was an important part of India's self-realization. "The spinning-wheel gradually became," as his biographer B.R. Nanda writes, "the center of rural uplift in the Gandhian scheme of Indian economics." Tagore found the alleged economic rationale for this scheme quite unrealistic. As Romain Rolland noted, Rabindranath "never tires of criticizing the charka." In this economic judgment, Tagore was probably right. Except for the rather small specialized market for high-quality spun cloth, it is hard to make economic sense of hand-spinning, even with wheels less primitive than Gandhi's charka. Hand-spinning as a widespread activity can survive only with the help of heavy government subsidies. However, Gandhi's advocacy of the charka was not based only on economics. He wanted everyone to spin for "thirty minutes every day as a sacrifice," seeing this as a way for people who are better off to identify themselves with the less fortunate. He was impatient with Tagore's refusal to grasp this point:

The poet lives for the morrow, and would have us do likewise.... "Why should I, who have no need to work for food, spin?" may be the question asked. Because I am eating what does not belong to me. I am living on the spoliation of my countrymen. Trace the source of every coin that finds its way into your pocket, and you will realise the truth of what I write.

Every one must spin. Let Tagore spin like the others. Let him burn his foreign clothes; that is the duty today. God will take care of the morrow.

If Tagore had missed something in Gandhi's argument, so did Gandhi miss the point of Tagore's main criticism. It was not only that the charka made little economic sense, but also, Tagore thought, that it was not the way to make people reflect on anything: "The charka does not require anyone to think; one simply turns the wheel of the antiquated invention endlessly, using the minimum of judgment and stamina."

Celibacy and Personal Life

Tagore and Gandhi's attitudes toward personal life were also quite different. Gandhi was keen on the virtues of celibacy, theorized about it, and, after some years of conjugal life, made a private commitment—publicly announced—to refrain from sleeping with his wife. Rabindranath's own attitude on this subject was very different, but he was gentle about their disagreements:

> *[Gandhiji] condemns sexual life as inconsistent with the moral progress of man, and has a horror of sex as great as that of the author of* The Kreutzer Sonata, *but, unlike Tolstoy, he betrays no abhorrence of the sex that tempts his kind. In fact, his tenderness for women is one of the noblest and most consistent traits of his character, and he counts among the women of his country some of his best and truest comrades in the great movement he is leading.*

Tagore's personal life was, in many ways, an unhappy one. He married in 1883, lost his wife in 1902, and never remarried. He sought close companionship, which he did not always get (perhaps even during his married life—he wrote to his wife, Mrinalini: "If you and I could be comrades in all our work and in all our thoughts it would be splendid, but we cannot attain all that we desire"). He maintained a warm friendship with, and a strong Platonic attachment to, the literature-loving wife, Kadambari, of his elder brother, Jyotirindranath. He dedicated some poems to her before his marriage, and several books afterward, some after her death (she committed suicide, for reasons that are not fully understood, at the age of twenty-five, four months after Rabindranath's wedding). Much later in life, during his tour of Argentina in 1924-1925, Rabindranath came to know the talented and beautiful Victoria Ocampo, who later became the publisher of the literary magazine *Sur.* They became close friends, but it appears that Rabindranath deflected the possibility of a passionate relationship into a confined intellectual one. His friend Leonard Elmhirst, who accompanied Rabindranath on his Argentine tour, wrote:

Besides having a keen intellectual understanding of his books, she was in love with him—but instead of being content to build a friendship on the basis of intellect, she was in a hurry to establish that kind of proprietary right over him which he absolutely would not brook.

Ocampo and Elmhirst, while remaining friendly, were both quite rude in what they wrote about each other. Ocampo's book on Tagore (of which a Bengali translation was made from the Spanish by the distinguished poet and critic Shankha Ghosh) is primarily concerned with Tagore's writings but also discusses the pleasures and difficulties of their relationship, giving quite a different account from Elmhirst's, and never suggesting any sort of proprietary intentions.

Victoria Ocampo, however, makes it clear that she very much wanted to get physically closer to Rabindranath: "Little by little he [Tagore] partially tamed the young animal, by turns wild and docile, who did not sleep, dog-like, on the floor outside his door, simply because it was not done." Rabindranath, too, was clearly very much attracted to her. He called her "Vijaya" (the Sanskrit equivalent of Victoria), dedicated a book of poems to her, Purabi—an "evening melody," and expressed great admiration for her mind ("like a star that was distant"). In a letter to her he wrote, as if to explain his own reticence:

When we were together, we mostly played with words and tried to laugh away our best opportunities to see each other clearly ... Whenever there is the least sign of the nest becoming a jealous rival of the sky [,] my mind, like a migrant bird, tries to take ... flight to a distant shore.

Five years later, during Tagore's European tour in 1930, he sent her a cable: "Will you not come and see me." She did. But their relationship did not seem to go much beyond conversation, and their somewhat ambiguous correspondence continued over the years. Written in 1940, a year before his death at eighty, one of the poems in Sesh Lekha ("Last Writings"), seems to be about her: "How I wish I could once again find my way to that foreign land where waits for me the message of love!/... Her language I knew not, but what her eyes said will forever remain eloquent in its anguish." However indecisive, or confused, or awkward Rabindranath may have been, he certainly did not share Mahatma Gandhi's censorious views of sex. In fact, when it came to social policy, he advocated contraception and family planning while Gandhi preferred abstinence.

Educational Ideas

Rabindranath Tagore's role in the innovation of educational ideas has been eclipsed by his fame as a poet. He was a pioneer in the field of education. For the last forty years of his life he was content to be a schoolmaster in humble rural surroundings, even when he had achieved fame such as no Indian had known before. He was one of the first, in India, to think out for himself and put in practice principles of education which have now become commonplace of educational theory, if not yet of practice.

Today we all know that what the child imbibes at home and in school is far more important than what he studies at college, that the teaching is more easily and naturally communicated through the child's mother-tongue than through an alien medium, that learning through activity is more real than through the written word, that wholesome education consists in training of all the senses along with the mind instead of cramming the brain with memorized knowledge, that culture is something much more than academic knowledge. But few of Rabindranath's countrymen took notice of him when he made his first experiments in education in 1901 with less than half a dozen pupils. A poet's whim, thought most of them. Even today few of his countrymen understand the significance of these principles in their national life. The schoolmaster is still the most neglected member of our community, despite the fact that Rabindranath attached more merit to what he taught to children in his school than to the Hibbert lectures he delivered before the distinguished audience at Oxfoard.

Mahatma Gandhi adopted the scheme of teaching through crafts many years after Rabindranath had worked it out at Santiniketan. In fact the Mahatma imported his first teachers for his basic School from Santiniketan. If Rabindranath had done nothing else, what he did at Santiniketan and Sriniketan would be sufficient to rank him as one of the India's greatest nation-builders.

With the years, Rabindranath had won the world and the world in turn had won him. He sought his home everywhere in the world and would bring the world to his home. And so the little school for children at Santiniketan became a world university, Visva-Bharati, a centre for Indian Culture, a seminary for Eastern Studies and a meeting-place of the East and West. The poet selected for its motto an ancient Sanskrit verse, *Yatra visvam bhavatieka nidam*, which means, "Where the whole world meets in a single nest."

> *"Visva-Bharati", he declared,* "represents India where she has her wealth of mind which is for all. Visva-Bharati acknowledges India's obligation to offer to others the hospitality of her best culture and India's right to accept from others their best."

In 1940 a year before he died, he put a letter in Gandhi's hand,

> *"Visva-Bharati is like a vessel which is carrying the cargo of my life's best treasure, and I hope it may claim special care from my countrymen for its preservation."*

Science and the People

Gandhi and Tagore severely clashed over their totally different attitudes toward science. In January 1934, Bihar was struck by a devastating earthquake, which killed thousands of people. Gandhi, who was then deeply involved in the fight against untouchability (the barbaric system inherited from India's divisive past, in which "lowly people" were kept at a physical distance), extracted a positive lesson from the tragic event. "A man like me," Gandhi argued, "cannot but believe this earthquake is a divine chastisement sent by God for our sins" — in particular the sins of untouchability. "For me there is a vital connection between the Bihar calamity and the untouchability campaign."

Tagore, who equally abhorred untouchability and had joined Gandhi in the movements against it, protested against this interpretation of an event that had caused suffering and death to so many innocent people, including children and babies. He also hated the epistemology implicit in seeing an earthquake as caused by ethical failure. "It is," he wrote, "all the more unfortunate because this kind of unscientific view of [natural] phenomena is too readily accepted by a large section of our countrymen."

The two remained deeply divided over their attitudes toward science. However, while Tagore believed that modern science was essential to the understanding of physical phenomena, his views on epistemology were interestingly heterodox. He did not take the simple "realist" position often associated with modern science. The report of his conversation with Einstein, published in The New York Times in 1930, shows how insistent Tagore was on interpreting truth through observation and reflective concepts.

To assert that something is true or untrue in the absence of anyone to observe or perceive its truth, or to form a conception of what it is, appeared to Tagore to be deeply questionable. When Einstein remarked, "If there were no human beings any more, the Apollo Belvedere no longer would be beautiful?" Tagore simply replied, "No." Going further—and into much more interesting territory—Einstein said, "I agree with regard to this conception of beauty, but not with regard to truth." Tagore's response was: "Why not? Truth is realized through men."

Tagore's epistemology, which he never pursued systematically, would seem to be searching for a line of reasoning that would later be elegantly developed by Hilary Putnam, who has argued: "Truth depends on conceptual schemes and it is nonetheless 'real truth.'" Tagore himself said little to explain his convictions, but it is important to take account of his heterodoxy, not only because his speculations were invariably interesting, but also because they illustrate how his support for any position, including his strong interest in science, was accompanied by critical scrutiny.

Nationalism and Colonialism

Tagore was predictably hostile to communal sectarianism (such as a Hindu orthodoxy that was antagonistic to Islamic, Christian, or Sikh perspectives). But even nationalism seemed to him to be suspect. Isaiah Berlin summarizes well Tagore's complex position on Indian nationalism:

Tagore stood fast on the narrow causeway, and did not betray his vision of the difficult truth. He condemned romantic overattachment to the past, what he called the tying of India to the past "like a sacrificial goat tethered to a post," and he accused men who displayed it - they seemed to him reactionary - of not knowing what true political freedom was, pointing out that it is from English thinkers and English books that the very notion of political liberty was derived. But against cosmopolitanism he maintained that the English stood on their own feet, and so must Indians. In 1917 he once more denounced the danger of 'leaving everything to the unalterable will of the Master,' be he Brahmin or Englishman.

The duality Berlin points to is well reflected also in Tagore's attitude toward cultural diversity. He wanted Indians to learn what is going on elsewhere, how others lived, what they valued, and so on, while remaining interested and involved in their own culture and heritage. Indeed, in his educational writings the need for synthesis is strongly stressed. It can also be found in his advice to Indian students abroad. In 1907 he wrote to his son-in-law Nagendranath Gangulee, who had gone to America to study agriculture: To get on familiar terms with the local people is a part of your education. To know only agriculture is not enough; you must know America too. Of course if, in the process of knowing America, one begins to lose one's identity and falls into the trap of becoming an Americanised person contemptuous of everything Indian, it is preferable to stay in a locked room.

Tagore was strongly involved in protest against the Raj on a number of occasions, most notably in the movement to resist the 1905 British proposal to split in two the province of Bengal, a plan that was eventually withdrawn following popular resistance. He was forthright in denouncing the brutality of British rule in India, never more so than after the Amritsar massacre of April 13, 1919, when 379 unarmed people at a peaceful meeting were gunned down by the army, and two thousand more were wounded. Between April 23 and 26, Rabindranath wrote five agitated letters to C.F. Andrews, who himself was extremely disturbed, especially after he was told by a British civil servant in India that thanks to this show of strength, the "moral prestige" of the Raj had "never been higher."

A month after the massacre, Tagore wrote to the Viceroy of India, asking to be relieved of the knighthood he had accepted four years earlier:

The disproportionate severity of the punishments inflicted upon the unfortunate people and the methods of carrying them out, we are convinced, are without parallel in the history of civilized governments, barring some conspicuous exceptions, recent and remote. Considering that such treatment has been meted out to a population, disarmed and resourceless, by a power which has the most terribly efficient organisation for destruction of human lives, we must strongly assert that it can claim no political expediency, far less moral justification.... The universal agony of indignation roused in the hearts of our people has been ignored by our rulers - possibly congratulating themselves for imparting what they imagine as salutary lessons.... I for my part want to stand, shorn of all special distinctions, by the side of those of my countrymen who for their so-called insignificance are liable to suffer a degradation not fit for human beings.

Both Gandhi and Nehru expressed their appreciation of the important part Tagore took in the national struggle. It is fitting that after independence, India chose a song of Tagore ("Jana Gana Mana Adhinayaka," which can be roughly translated as "the leader of people's minds") as its national anthem. Since Bangladesh would later choose another song of Tagore ("Amar Sonar Bangla") as its national anthem, he may be the only one ever to have authored the national anthems of two different countries.

Tagore's criticism of the British administration of India was consistently strong and grew more intense over the years. This point is often missed, since he made a special effort to dissociate his criticism of the Raj from any denigration of British—or Western—people and culture. Mahatma Gandhi's well-known quip in reply to a question, asked in England, on what he thought of Western civilization ("It would be a good idea") could not have come from Tagore's lips. He would understand the provocations to which Gandhi was responding - involving cultural conceit as well as imperial tyranny. D.H. Lawrence supplied a fine example of the former: "I become more and more surprised to see how far higher, in reality, our European civilization stands than the East, Indian and Persian, ever dreamed of.... This fraud of looking up to them—this wretched worship-of-Tagore attitude is disgusting." But, unlike Gandhi, Tagore could not, even in jest, be dismissive of Western civilization.

Even in his powerful indictment of British rule in India in 1941, in a lecture which he gave on his last birthday, and which was later published as a pamphlet under the title *Crisis in Civilization,* he strains hard to maintain the distinction between opposing Western imperialism and rejecting Western civilization. While he saw India as having been "smothered under the dead weight of British administration" (adding "another great and ancient civilization for whose recent tragic history the British cannot disclaim responsibility is China"), Tagore recalls what India has gained from "discussions centred upon Shakespeare's drama and Byron's poetry and above all...the large-hearted liberalism of nineteenth-century English politics." The tragedy, as Tagore saw it, came from the fact that what "was truly best in their own civilization, the upholding of dignity of human relationships, has no place in the British administration of this country." "If in its place they have established, baton in hand, a reign of 'law and order,' or in other words a policeman's rule, such a mockery of civilization can claim no respect from us."

Critique of Patriotism

Rabindranath rebelled against the strongly nationalist form that the independence movement often took, and this made him refrain from taking a particularly active part in contemporary politics. He wanted to assert India's right to be independent without denying the importance of what India could learn—freely and profitably—from abroad. He was afraid that a rejection of the West in favor of an indigenous Indian tradition was not only limiting in itself; it could easily turn into hostility to other influences from abroad, including Christianity, which came to parts of India by the fourth century; Judaism, which came through Jewish immigration shortly after the fall of Jerusalem, as did Zoroastrianism through Parsi immigration later on (mainly in the eighth century), and, of course—and most importantly—Islam, which has had a very strong presence in India since the tenth century.

Tagore's criticism of patriotism is a persistent theme in his writings. As early as 1908, he put his position succinctly in a letter replying to the criticism of Abala Bose, the wife of a great Indian scientist, Jagadish Chandra Bose: "Patriotism cannot be our final spiritual shelter; my refuge is humanity. I will not buy glass for the price of diamonds, and I will never allow patriotism to triumph over humanity as long as I live." His novel *Ghare Baire* (The Home and the World) has much to say about this theme. In the novel, Nikhil, who is keen on social reform, including women's liberation, but cool toward nationalism, gradually loses the esteem of his spirited wife, Bimala, because of his failure to be enthusiastic about anti-British agitations, which she sees as a lack of patriotic commitment. Bimala becomes fascinated with Nikhil's nationalist friend Sandip, who speaks brilliantly and acts with patriotic militancy, and she falls in love with him. Nikhil refuses to change his views: "I am willing to serve my country; but my worship I reserve for Right which is far greater than my country. To worship my country as a god is to bring a curse upon it."

As the story unfolds, Sandip becomes angry with some of his countrymen for their failure to join the struggle as readily as he thinks they should ("Some Mohamedan traders are still obdurate"). He arranges to deal with the recalcitrants by burning their meager trading stocks and physically attacking them. Bimala has to acknowledge the connection between Sandip's rousing nationalistic sentiments and his sectarian - and ultimately violent-actions. The dramatic events that follow (Nikhil attempts to help the victims, risking his life) include the end of Bimala's political romance.

This is a difficult subject, and Satyajit Ray's beautiful film of *The Home and the World* brilliantly brings out the novel's tensions, along with the human affections and disaffections of the story. Not surprisingly, the story has had many detractors, not just among dedicated nationalists in India. George Lukács found Tagore's novel to be "a petit bourgeois yarn of the shoddiest kind," "at the intellectual service of the British police," and "a contemptible caricature of Gandhi." It would, of course, be absurd to think of Sandip as Gandhi, but the novel gives a "strong and gentle" warning, as Bertolt Brecht noted in his diary, of the corruptibility of nationalism, since it is not even-handed. Hatred of one group can lead to hatred of others, no matter how far such feeling may be from the minds of large-hearted nationalist leaders like Mahatma Gandhi.

Admiration and Criticism of Japan

Tagore's reaction to nationalism in Japan is particularly telling. As in the case of India, he saw the need to build the self-confidence of a defeated and humiliated people, of people left behind by developments elsewhere, as was the case in Japan before its emergence during the nineteenth century. At the beginning of one of his lectures in Japan in 1916 ("Nationalism in Japan"), he observed that "the worst form of bondage is the bondage of dejection, which keeps men hopelessly chained in loss of faith in themselves." Tagore shared the admiration for Japan widespread in Asia for demonstrating the ability of an Asian nation to rival the West in industrial development and economic progress. He noted with great satisfaction that Japan had "in giant strides left centuries of inaction behind, overtaking the present time in its foremost achievement." For other nations outside the West, he said, Japan "has broken the spell under which we lay in torpor for ages, taking it to be the normal condition of certain races living in certain geographical limits."

But then Tagore went on to criticize the rise of a strong nationalism in Japan, and its emergence as an imperialist nation. Tagore's outspoken criticisms did not please Japanese audiences and, as E.P. Thompson wrote, "the welcome given to him on his first arrival soon cooled." Twenty-two years later, in 1937, during the Japanese war on China, Tagore received a letter from Rash Behari Bose, an anti-British Indian revolutionary then living in Japan, who sought Tagore's approval for his efforts there on behalf of Indian independence, in which he had the support of the Japanese government. Tagore replied:

Your cable has caused me many restless hours, for it hurts me very much to have to ignore your appeal. I wish you had asked for my cooperation in a cause against which my spirit did not protest. I know, in making this appeal, you counted on my great regard for the Japanese for I, along with the rest of Asia, did once admire and look up to Japan and did once fondly hope that in Japan Asia had at last discovered its challenge to the West, that Japan's new strength would be consecrated in safeguarding the culture of the East against alien interests. But Japan has not taken long to betray that rising hope and repudiate all that seemed significant in her wonderful, and, to us symbolic, awakening, and has now become itself a worse menace to the defenceless peoples of the East.

How to view Japan's position in the Second World War was a divisive issue in India. After the war, when Japanese political leaders were tried for war crimes, the sole dissenting voice among the judges came from the Indian judge, Radhabinod Pal, a distinguished jurist. Pal dissented on various grounds, among them that no fair trial was possible in view of the asymmetry of power between the victor and the defeated. Ambivalent feelings in India toward the Japanese military aggression, given the unacceptable nature of British imperialism, possibly had a part in predisposing Pal to consider a perspective different from that of the other judges.

More tellingly, Subhash Chandra Bose (no relation of Rash Behari Bose), a leading nationalist, made his way to Japan during the war via Italy and Germany after escaping from a British prison; he helped the Japanese to form units of Indian soldiers, who had earlier surrendered to the advancing Japanese army, to fight on the Japanese side as the "Indian National Army." Rabindranath had formerly entertained great admiration for Subhas Bose as a dedicated nonsectarian fighter for Indian independence. But their ways would have parted when Bose's political activities took this turn, although Tagore was dead by the time Bose reached Japan.

Tagore saw Japanese militarism as illustrating the way nationalism can mislead even a nation of great achievement and promise. In 1938 Yone Noguchi, the distinguished poet and friend of Tagore (as well as of Yeats and Pound), wrote to Tagore, pleading with him to change his mind about Japan. Rabindranath's reply, written on September 12, 1938, was altogether uncompromising:

It seems to me that it is futile for either of us to try to convince the other, since your faith in the infallible right of Japan to bully other Asiatic nations into line with your Government's policy is not shared by me.... Believe me, it is sorrow and shame, not anger, that prompt me to write to you. I suffer intensely not only because the reports of Chinese suffering batter against my heart, but because I can no longer point out with pride the example of a great Japan.

He would have been much happier with the postwar emergence of Japan as a peaceful power. Then, too, since he was not free of egotism, he would also have been pleased by the attention paid to his ideas by the novelist Yasunari Kawabata and others.

International Concerns

Tagore was not invariably well-informed about international politics. He allowed himself to be entertained by Mussolini in a short visit to Italy in May-June 1926, a visit arranged by Carlo Formichi, professor of Sanskrit at the University of Rome. When he asked to meet Benedetto Croce, Formichi said, "Impossible! Impossible!" Mussolini told him that Croce was "not in Rome." When Tagore said he would go "wherever he is," Mussolini assured him that Croce's whereabouts were unknown.

Such incidents, as well as warnings from Romain Rolland and other friends, should have ended Tagore's flirtation with Mussolini more quickly than it did. But only after he received graphic accounts of the brutality of Italian fascism from two exiles, Gaetano Salvemini and Gaetano Salvadori, and learned more of what was happening in Italy, did he publicly denounce the regime, publishing a letter to the *Manchester Guardian* in August. The next month, Popolo d'Italia, the magazine edited by Benito Mussolini's brother, replied: "Who cares? Italy laughs at Tagore and those who brought this unctuous and insupportable fellow in our midst."

With his high expectations of Britain, Tagore continued to be surprised by what he took to be a lack of official sympathy for international victims of aggression. He returned to this theme in the lecture he gave on his last birthday, in 1941:

While Japan was quietly devouring North China, her act of wanton aggression was ignored as a minor incident by the veterans of British diplomacy. We have also witnessed from this distance how actively the British statesmen acquiesced in the destruction of the Spanish Republic.

But distinguishing between the British government and the British people, Rabindranath went on to note "with admiration how a band of valiant Englishmen laid down their lives for Spain."

Tagore's view of the Soviet Union has been a subject of much discussion. He was widely read in Russia. In 1917 several Russian translations of *Gitanjali* (one edited by Ivan Bunin, later the first Russian Nobel Laureate in Literature) were available, and by the late 1920s many of the English versions of his work had been rendered into Russian by several distinguished translators. Russian versions of his work continued to appear: Boris Pasternak translated him in the 1950s and 1960s.

When Tagore visited Russia in 1930, he was much impressed by its development efforts and by what he saw as a real commitment to eliminate poverty and economic inequality. But what impressed him most was the expansion of basic education across the old Russian empire. In Letters from Russia, written in Bengali and published in 1931, he unfavorably compares the acceptance of widespread illiteracy in India by the British administration with Russian efforts to expand education:

In stepping on the soil of Russia, the first thing that caught my eye was that in education, at any rate, the peasant and the working classes have made such enormous progress in these few years that nothing comparable has happened even to our highest classes in the course of the last hundred and fifty years.... The people here are not at all afraid of giving complete education even to Turcomans of distant Asia; on the contrary, they are utterly in earnest about it.

When parts of the book were translated into English in 1934, the under-secretary for India stated in Parliament that it was "calculated by distortion of the facts to bring the British Administration in India into contempt and disrepute," and the book was then promptly banned. The English version would not be published until after independence.

Education and Freedom

The British Indian administrators were not, however, alone in trying to suppress Tagore's reflections on Russia. They were joined by Soviet officials. In an interview with *Izvestia* in 1930, Tagore sharply criticized the lack of freedom that he observed in Russia:

I must ask you: Are you doing your ideal a service by arousing in the minds of those under your training anger, class-hatred, and revengefulness against those whom you consider to be your enemies?... Freedom of mind is needed for the reception of truth; terror hopelessly kills it.... For the sake of humanity I hope you may never create a vicious force of violence, which will go on weaving an interminable chain of violence and cruelty.... You have tried to destroy many of the other evils of [the czarist] period. Why not try to destroy this one also?

The interview was not published in *Izvestia* until 1988—nearly sixty years later. Tagore's reaction to the Russia of 1930 arose from two of his strongest commitments: his uncompromising belief in the importance of "freedom of mind" (the source of his criticism of the Soviet Union), and his conviction that the expansion of basic education is central to social progress (the source of his praise, particularly in contrast to British-run India). He identified the lack of basic education as the fundamental cause of many of India's social and economic afflictions:

In my view the imposing tower of misery which today rests on the heart of India has its sole foundation in the absence of education. Caste divisions, religious conflicts, aversion to work, precarious economic conditions - all centre on this single factor.

It was on education (and on the reflection, dialogue, and communication that are associated with it), rather than on, say, spinning "as a sacrifice" ("the charka does not require anyone to think"), that the future of India would depend.

Tagore was concerned not only that there be wider opportunities for education across the country (especially in rural areas where schools were few), but also that the schools themselves be more lively and enjoyable. He himself had dropped out of school early, largely out of boredom, and had never bothered to earn a diploma. He wrote extensively on how schools should be made more attractive to boys and girls and thus more productive. His own co-educational school at Santiniketan had many progressive features. The emphasis here was on self-motivation rather than on discipline, and on fostering intellectual curiosity rather than competitive excellence.

Much of Rabindranath's life was spent in developing the school at Santiniketan. The school never had much money, since the fees were very low. His lecture honoraria, "$700 a scold," went to support it, as well as most of his Nobel Prize money. The school received no support from the government, but did get help from private citizens—even Mahatma Gandhi raised money for it.

The dispute with Mahatma Gandhi on the Bihar earthquake touched on a subject that was very important to Tagore: the need for education in science as well as in literature and the humanities. At Santiniketan, there were strong "local" elements in its emphasis on Indian traditions, including the classics, and in the use of Bengali rather than English as the language of instruction. At the same time there were courses on a great variety of cultures, and study programs devoted to China, Japan, and the Middle East. Many foreigners came to Santiniketan to study or teach, and the fusion of studies seemed to work.

I am partial to seeing Tagore as an educator, having myself been educated at Santiniketan. The school was unusual in many different ways, such as the oddity that classes, excepting those requiring a laboratory, were held outdoors (whenever the weather permitted). No matter what we thought of Rabindranath's belief that one gains from being in a natural setting while learning (some of us argued about this theory), we typically found the experience of outdoor schooling extremely attractive and pleasant. Academically, our school was not particularly exacting (often we did not have any examinations at all), and it could not, by the usual academic standards, compete with some of the better schools in Calcutta.

But there was something remarkable about the ease with which class discussions could move from Indian traditional literature to contemporary as well as classical Western thought, and then to the culture of China or Japan or elsewhere. The school's celebration of variety was also in sharp contrast with the cultural conservatism and separatism that has tended to grip India from time to time.

The cultural give and take of Tagore's vision of the contemporary world has close parallels with the vision of Satyajit Ray, also an alumnus of Santiniketan who made several films based on Tagore's stories. Ray's words about Santiniketan in 1991 would have greatly pleased Rabindranath:

I consider the three years I spent in Santiniketan as the most fruitful of my life.... Santiniketan opened my eyes for the first time to the splendours of Indian and Far Eastern art. Until then I was completely under the sway of Western art, music and literature. Santiniketan made me the combined product of East and West that I am.

India Today

At the fiftieth anniversary of Indian independence, the reckoning of what India had or had not achieved in this half century was a subject of considerable interest: "What has been the story of those first fifty years?" (as Shashi Tharoor asked in his balanced, informative, and highly readable account of *India: From Midnight to the Millennium*). If Tagore were to see the India of today, more than half a century after independence, nothing perhaps would shock him so much as the continued illiteracy of the masses. He would see this as a total betrayal of what the nationalist leaders had promised during the struggle for independence—a promise that had figured even in Nehru's rousing speech on the eve of independence in August 1947 (on India's "tryst with destiny").

In view of his interest in childhood education, Tagore would not be consoled by the extraordinary expansion of university education, in which India sends to its universities six times as many people per unit of population as does China. Rather, he would be stunned that, in contrast to East and Southeast Asia, including China, half the adult population and two thirds of Indian women remain unable to read or write. Statistically reliable surveys indicate that even in the late 1980s, nearly half of the rural girls between the ages of twelve and fourteen did not attend any school for a single day of their lives.

This state of affairs is the result of the continuation of British imperial neglect of mass education, which has been reinforced by India's traditional elitism, as well as upper-class-dominated contemporary politics (except in parts of India such as Kerala, where anti-upper-caste movements have tended to concentrate on education as a great leveller). Tagore would see illiteracy and the neglect of education not only as the main source of India's continued social backwardness, but also as a great constraint that restricts the possibility and reach of economic development in India (as his writings on rural development forcefully make clear). Tagore would also have strongly felt the need for a greater commitment—and a greater sense of urgency—in removing endemic poverty.

At the same time, Tagore would undoubtedly find some satisfaction in the survival of democracy in India, in its relatively free press, and in general from the "freedom of mind" that post-independence Indian politics has, on the whole, managed to maintain. He would also be pleased by the fact noted by the historian E.P. Thompson (whose father Edward Thompson had written one of the first major biographies of Tagore:

All the convergent influences of the world run through this society: Hindu, Moslem, Christian, secular; Stalinist, liberal, Maoist, democratic socialist, Gandhian. There is not a thought that is being thought in the West or East that is not active in some Indian mind.

Tagore would have been happy also to see that the one governmental attempt to dispense generally with basic liberties and political and civil rights in India, in the 1970s, when Prime Minister Indira Gandhi (ironically, herself a former student at Santiniketan) declared an "emergency," was overwhelmingly rejected by the Indian voters, leading to the precipitate fall of her government.

Rabindranath would also see that the changes in policy that have eliminated famine since independence had much to do with the freedom to be heard in a democratic India. In Tagore's play *Raja O Rani* ("The King and the Queen"), the sympathetic Queen eventually rebels against the callousness of state policy toward the hungry. She begins by inquiring about the ugly sounds outside the palace, only to be told that the noise is coming from "the coarse, clamorous crowd who howl unashamedly for food and disturb the sweet peace of the palace." The Viceregal office in India could have taken a similarly callous view of Indian famines, right up to the easily preventable Bengal famine of 1943, just before independence, which killed between two and three million people. But a government in a multi-party democracy, with elections and free newspapers, cannot any longer dismiss the noise from "the coarse, clamorous crowd."

Unlike Gandhi, Rabindranath would not resent the development of modern industries in India, or the acceleration of technical progress, since he did not want India to be shackled to the turning of "the wheel of an antiquated invention." Tagore was concerned that people not be dominated by machines, but he was not opposed to making good use of modern technology.

"The mastery over the machine," he wrote in *Crisis in Civilization,* "by which the British have consolidated their sovereignty over their vast empire, has been kept a sealed book, to which due access has been denied to this helpless country." Rabindranath had a deep interest in the environment - he was particularly concerned about deforestation and initiated a "festival of tree-planting" (vriksha-ropana) as early as 1928. He would want increased private and government commitments to environmentalism; but he would not derive from this position a general case against modern industry and technology.

On Cultural Separation

Rabindranath would be shocked by the growth of cultural separatism in India, as elsewhere. The "openness" that he valued so much is certainly under great strain right now - in many countries. Religious fundamentalism still has a relatively small following in India; but various factions seem to be doing their best to increase their numbers. Certainly religious sectarianism has had much success in some parts of India (particularly in the west and the north). Tagore would see the expansion of religious sectarianism as being closely associated with an artificially separatist view of culture.

He would have strongly resisted defining India in specifically Hindu terms, rather than as a "confluence" of many cultures. Even after the partition of 1947, India is still the third- largest Muslim country in the world, with more Muslims than in Bangladesh, and nearly as many as in Pakistan. Only Indonesia has substantially more followers of Islam. Indeed, by pointing to the immense heterogeneousness of India's cultural background and its richly diverse history, Tagore had argued that the "idea of India" itself militated against a culturally separatist view—"against the intense consciousness of the separateness of one's own people from others."

Tagore would also oppose the cultural nationalism that has recently been gaining some ground in India, along with an exaggerated fear of the influence of the West. He was uncompromising in his belief that human beings could absorb quite different cultures in constructive ways:

Whatever we understand and enjoy in human products instantly becomes ours, wherever they might have their origin. I am proud of my humanity when I can acknowledge the poets and artists of other countries as my own. Let me feel with unalloyed gladness that all the great glories of man are mine. Therefore it hurts me deeply when the cry of rejection rings loud against the West in my country with the clamour that Western education can only injure us.

In this context, it is important to emphasize that Rabindranath was not short of pride in India's own heritage, and often spoke about it. He lectured at Oxford, with evident satisfaction, on the importance of India's religious ideas—quoting both from ancient texts and from popular poetry (such as the verses of the sixteenth-century Muslim poet Kabir). In 1940, when he was given an honorary doctorate by Oxford University, in a ceremony arranged at his own educational establishment in Santiniketan ("In Gangem Defluit Isis," Oxford helpfully explained), to the predictable "volley of Latin" Tagore responded "by a volley of Sanskrit," as Marjorie Sykes, a Quaker friend of Rabindranath, reports. Her cheerful summary of the match, "India held its own," was not out of line with Tagore's pride in Indian culture. His welcoming attitude to Western civilization was reinforced by this confidence: he did not see India's culture as fragile and in need of "protection" from Western influence.

In India, he wrote, "circumstances almost compel us to learn English, and this lucky accident has given us the opportunity of access into the richest of all poetical literatures of the world." There seems to me much force in Rabindranath's argument for clearly distinguishing between the injustice of a serious asymmetry of power (colonialism being a prime example of this) and the importance nevertheless of appraising Western culture in an open-minded way, in colonial and postcolonial territories, in order to see what uses could be made of it.

Rabindranath insisted on open debate on every issue, and distrusted conclusions based on a mechanical formula, no matter how attractive that formula might seem in isolation (such as "This was forced on us by our colonial masters - we must reject it," "This is our tradition—we must follow it," "We have promised to do this—we must fulfil that promise," and so on). The question he persistently asks is whether we have reason enough to want what is being proposed, taking everything into account. Important as history is, reasoning has to go beyond the past. It is in the sovereignty of reasoning—fearless reasoning in freedom—that we can find Rabindranath Tagore's lasting voice.

Devotio Humana: Rabindranath's Love Poems Revisited

I Rabindranath Tagore's (1861-1941) reputation as a *rishi* (saint), *mahamanab* (superman), or *gurudeb* (divine mentor) has created a haze and a halo through which we can neither recognize the concrete human being of flesh and blood nor appreciate his emotional sensibilities in their proper perspectives. As such, a number of critics such as Ajitkumar Chakravarti, Srikumar Banerjee, Mohitlal Majumdar, or Charuchandra Banerjee either refused to consider the direct influence of the human experiences, especially his relationships with various women, on some of Rabindranath's greatest lyrical pieces, or considered any attempt to probe into them irrelevant, irreverent, or irresponsible. However, the distinguished Tagore scholar Pramathanath Bishi provided an explanation for his claim that Rabindranath's poems and lyrics dealing with love lack human intimacy. A distinct signature of Tagore's love poems, Bishi goes on, is that they reveal sadness, disappointment, and compassion rather than passion, euphoria, or tumult of the heart.

If we pay heed to Buddhadeva Bose and Sankha Ghosh's sensible suggestion to read Rabindranath's poetry *qua* poetry *(kabitar uddeshe kabita)* and try not to analyze it either insisting on the contexts and causes of his works or ignoring their human and historical but emphasizing spiritual or philosophical dimensions, we would readily realize that he truly was what another great poet of his day, though hailing from an earlier generation, Walt Whitman of America (1819-92), wrote in a celebrated poem: "I am large, I contain multitudes." Indeed, as Tagore has clearly stated, "human mind is deep and variegated ; swayed by multiple pulls and pressures it has to bend [and adjust]. That is the sign of its life, its humanity, and its protests against sterile immobility. One who does not face this ambivalence and weakness has a very narrow, hard, and dead mind. Our instinct, which we ridicule often, is the motor of life, it elevates us unto the infinite through pain and pleasure, sanctity and sin." Yet, beneath all his contradictions and ambivalence in respect of a number of issues there is a strong undercurrent of Rabindranath's essential humanism that was nurtured by his native culture he inherited and the Western culture of his day he imbibed. Nothing illustrates this problematic of Tagore's "myriad-minded" genius more clearly and wonderfully than his poems dealing with love.

Admittedly, this paper does not pretend to posit an entirely novel interpretation of Tagore's poems and lyrics dealing with love. On the other hand, the following pages bring together insights of several distinguished studies in Bengali to highlight the profile of Rabindranath, the sensitive, sensuous, shy as well as a spiritual human being. Tagore's delicate and refined sensibilities dictated his poetic imagination and public discourse and his entire life was dedicated to celebrate the beautiful and the eternal and proclaim the triumph of human love sublimated in cosmic compassion and agape or divine love. In fact, the poet himself confessed to his own fluid understanding of love in a letter to Pramatha Chaudhuri, husband of Tagore's beloved niece Indira : "I can't tell for sure whether I am driven by [human] love with all its pleasures and pain deriving from union and separation [of lovers] or by an indefinite but inordinate longing for beauty." As early as 1891, Rabindranath had written a poem on *prem* [love]: *"E ye sakhi, hridayer prem—/ Sukhduhkhabedanar adianta nahi yar,/Chiradainya, chirapurna hem./. . . bujha yai adho prem, adhkhana mon—/Samasta ke bujhechhe kakhan?"* [This love of mine springs from the heart./It has limitless pangs and pleasures, always empty, always filled with pure gold./...It's easy to figure out a little love or a bit of the heart's desires,/But who could fathom the depth of love in its fullness and entirety?]

II Any discussion of Rabindranath's concept of erotic love, that is *prem,* must be prefaced by and predicated on his understanding of human love as well as his outlook on the feminine. Jagadish Bhattacharya has discussed in detail the Hindu cultural influences of the Tagore family (even though Brahmo) and the Western intellectual influences of Renaissance Bengal where Rabindranath was born and brought up. The young poet at once internalized the *parakiya* prem [love without lust or *niskam prem*] of the Vaishnab *sahajiyas* represented by the fourteenth-century poet Chandidas as well as the *eros* of Plato (427-347 B.C.) via the *corpus* of Tagore's predecessor in England the "natural Platonist" Percy B. Shelley (1792-1822), the love of Dante Alighieri (1265-1321) expressed for Beatrice Portinari (1266-90) in *La Vita Nuova,* or that of Francesco Petrarca (1304-74) expressed for Laura de Noves (1308-48) in *Canzoniere.* Rabindranath himself admitted to his attraction for the poet John Keats (1795-1821) in an essay in 1895: "Of all the English poets known to me, I feel an especial intimacy with Keats ... [whose] language is marked by a sincere aesthetic delight."

Buddhadeva Bose argues persuasively that Tagore's collection of poems in *Manasi* constitutes the primary *locus* or an "atomic world" *("anubishwa")* of the poet's lyrical *ouevres* and their *leitmotif* is love. Bose argues further that the object of Tagore's love poems in *Manasi* [Woman of Imagination, 1890] is not a concrete identifiable individual but an indefinite fluid entity. At best, as Bose concludes, "most of [Tagore's] poems beginning with *Manasi* down to *Gitanjali* [Song Offerings, 1906-10] are ambivalent or multivalent in that their subject matter love cannot be said to be love in human or divine sense with any certainty."

According to another distinguished Tagore scholar, Kshudiram Das, Rabindranath's literary genius consists, fundamentally, in his assimilation of visible real life *(jiban)* with the idealized or imagined unseen *(arup)* that transcends the sensate world. This synthesis is a reflection of the poet's successful amalgam of the sensuous Western literary tradition and the introspective meditative tradition of his native culture. While Das perhaps comes closer to truth, he tends to overlook the human experiences that inspired some of the poet's outstanding creations in a major way. In the final analysis we must recognize the vast inclusive expanse of his *Weltanschauung* that comprehends a multiplicity of perspectives and trajectories defying any straitjacketed categories.

III It must also be noted that Rabindranath's upbringing in a spartan, though never overly puritan, Brahmo family might have conditioned him against any outward expression of emotional outbursts or sexuality. He never experienced any parental indulgence as a child being neither the eldest nor the youngest. His movements inside as well as outside the home were restricted. Admittedly, he was not neglected but, in keeping with the usual practice of his day, as a child he was kept away from the adult world under the control of the household servants, especially the two redoubtable veterans Brajeshwar and Shyam. From his boyhood, Rabindranath learnt to live a simple but disciplined life. "It could be said that luxury was conspicuous by its absence in our childhood," Tagore recalled later. He wrote elsewhere: "I was a lonely child, I had no friends to play with. But I had the great big visible world to keep me company." He had been a sparse eater, though he did take part in physical exercise on a daily basis. He, however, disliked attending school as he must have found the atmosphere there boring and choking.

At the same time, he was subjected to a strict regimen of studies and musical lessons at home under private tutors.

His evolution into adulthood occurred under such a controlled environment. The Brahmo etiquette of his family permitted free mixing between male and female members under certain parameters that were neither wholly patriarchal nor entirely egalitarian in terms of genders. Even as a mature young man Tagore manifested his uneasiness in female company. Admiring his young England-educated nephew Surendranath's spontaneous socialization with young women *(besh ritimata paka styley alap),* the thirty-two year old poet confessed: "Even at 32 I am unable to converse with women in such an easy, self-assured, and elegant manner. I stumble while walking, fumble while talking, and I am at a loss as to where to place hands or what to do with my long legs; while thus preoccupied with them I fail to continue conversations [with women] satisfactorily. In a crowded room [dimly] lit by three candles it becomes impossible for a clumsy and cowardly creature like me to get myself close to a young woman like iron to a magnet."

No wonder the young Rabindranath failed to summon a typical masculine response to the Maratha belle Anna Tadkhad's unabashed but sincere gesture to get him to hug and kiss her. Many years later, the poet confessed to his timid unromantic indifference to the pretty Anna's (he had nicknamed her "Nalini") overtures. He was similarly unresponsive to the erotic advances of the Scott sisters of Bloomsbury, London where the young poet had been a paying guest. As he told Dilip Ray many years later, he had little doubt that the girls, his "lovers in former life" *(purba janamer priya),* really fell for him and yet we notice his shy behavior at the initial stage of his meeting with them; he could not even summon the courage to look at one of them, Miss J, straight in the eye, lest he should lose his cool beholding her "well-chiseled countenance" *[apurba chhanche dhala mukh].* The poet's experiences with the mature, independent-minded, and intellectual Victoria Ocampo (1891-1979) of Argentina, whom he named Bijaya (a Bengali synonym for Victoria), register a similar episode of unrequited passion. One might reasonably suppose that his intimacy with Kadambari (1858-84), wife of his elder brother Jyotirindranath (1849-1925), was immaculate—it being a romantic communion or (as will be discussed later, *bhalobasa*) because of a tabooed relationship.

Kadambari had possessed the poet's heart by gifting away hers to him. In fact Tagore dedicated a number of poems to her: *Bhagnahriday* (Heartbreak, 1881), *Chhabi O Gaan* (Images and Lyrics, 1884), *Prakritir Pratishodh* (Nature's Revenge, 1884), *Shaishab Sangeet* (Song of Childhood, 1884), *Bhanusingha Thakurer Padabali* (Lyrics by Bhanusingha Thakur, 1884), and the like. Victoria Ocampo, on the other hand, fell in love hook, line and sinker with a handsome sexagenarian fit to be her father in age, and she did not hide her feelings for her *gurudeb.* "I love you. Nothing can alter that," she confessed candidly in one of her missives to the master and concluded reiterating her feelings for him: "let me tell you, Gurudev, that I love you". The old bard in turn dedicated his anthology *Purabi* (1925) to his Argentine adorer Bijaya. As he recalled his enchanted encounter: *Bidesher bhalobasa diye/ Ye preyasi petechhe asan/Chiradin rakhibe bandhiya/Kane kane tahari bhasan./Bhasa yar jana chhila nako,/Ankhi yar kayechhila katha,/Jagaye rakhibe chiradin/Sakarun tahari barata* [The lover who has gifted a throne/ with her love from a strange land,/Her whisperings will ring in (my) ears/For all time to come./Her language I did not know/Only her eyes spoke to me./Her melancholy message will endure for all time to come]. Ketaki Kushari Dyson, who has admirably probed into Ocampo's relationship with the aging Rabindranath in 1924-25, maintains that she became a Muse for the poet's creative corpus after 1924.

Dyson's claims for Ocampo's impact on Rabindranath's literary output since the mid 1920s conflict with Bhattacharya's observations on the influence of the precocious child Ranu Adhikari (later Lady Ranu Mukherjee), whose beauty, simplicity, and gloriously freewheeling love and admiration for the handsome old man inspired his creative genius in significant ways. The child Ranu appeared as the messenger of the poet's *Jibandebata* reminding him of the playmate of his early youth

Kadambari—"morning star of his life transformed into the evening star [of his old age]" *(bhorer tara elo sanhjher tarar beshe).* Even Tagore's younger relatives wondered about the "new inspiration" and "cause" of the "outpouring of new poems of a fine and noble vintage." There were other women in the poet's life—less glamorous intellectually—who impacted his psyche and work, women such as his child-bride Mrinalini (though more a spouse than a Muse), his niece Indira, his sister-in-law Jnadanandini, his daughter-in-law Pratima, his granddaughter Nandita, and Rani Mahalanabis, and Rani Chanda.

When we examine the various stages in Tagore's understanding and appreciation of woman's humanity, we cannot fail to notice that while as an adolescent, he saw her as a fairy queen of his dream world; as a young man he saw her as a romantic princess. Naturally, women awakened his unbridled youthful passion; witness his output during 1878-84. For instance, his *Kabikahini* [A Poet's Lore] and *Banaphool* [Wild Flowers], the two novellas in verse, published in 1878 and 1880 respectively, with their theme of an intimate relationship between femininity and the natural world, express the poet's spontaneous lyrical genius but contain a mishmash of wishy-washy sentimental excesses. Recalling *Bhagnahriday,* Tagore himself observed later that at the time of composing this piece his mind was filled with vaporous bubble and his sentimental gunk was being churned in the whirlpool of fantasies without any purpose. This was sterile stirring—devoid of creativity and beauty. His lack of direction and aimless amorous fantasy yielded to intensely passionate longings especially in pieces such as *Asahay Bhalobasa* (Unbearable Passion), *Ami Hara* (Loss of 'I'), *Upahar* (Gift), and *Durdin* (Hard Times), all belonging to the collection titled *Sandhya Sangeet* [Evening Song, 1882] . The young poet's heart was shivering in trepidation having been overcome by an uncontrollable longing for the bliss of a mysterious woman's touch: *"Man mor pagaler hena/ Pranpane shudhay se yena,/Praner majhe ki karile tomare go pai,/Ye thnai rayechhe shunya ki karile se shunya purai"* (My ecstatic heart seeks you in daring desperation,/Asking how could I get near you, how [could I] fill the void [in my heart] that you created). As he confided to Pramatha Chaudhuri: "I passed the whole day [during the period of the composition of *Chhabi O Gaan* [Pictures and Songs] like a lunatic—I was overwhelmed by the gushing flood tide of my newly awakened youth."

By the time Rabindranath composed the poems of *Chhabi O Gaan,* he had crossed the boundary of dreamy and idealized romantic longings of adolescence and entered the tumultuous world of youth assailed by an intense feeling of adult erotic urge. Unlike the earlier mood of his adolescence, when he sought the abstract and idealized woman of his fancy, the fully grown young man now set out to construct the image of a realistic female. As he recalled the period of the composition of *Chhabi O Gan* in his old age, his "desire [for a woman's love] was not to be satisfied with mere music, he now wished to savor her physical beauty." This state of mind is made lyrically manifest in the piece that cries out loud: *Hridaye jagaye basanar shikha/Nayane sajaye maya marichika/Shudhu ghure mari marubhume/Tabu kena, tabu kena michhe e pipasa./Biswa-charachara lupta haye yay/E ki ghor prem andharahu pray/ Jibana-youbana grase/Tabe kena, tabe kena michhe e kuyasa.* [I move about aimlessly with my heart burning in desire/And my eyes beholding an illusive mirage./ What, then, my love is for?/This tremendous passion, like the blinding *Rahu,* consumes my youth and my life./Why, then, is this love of mine?] (*Mayar Khela* [Play of Maya], 1888). Such anxious longings and ecstatic excitement mark his poems, *inter alia,* "Nirjharer Swapnabhanga" [The Awakening of the Waterfall], and "Ananta Jiban" [Eternal Life], all belonging to the anthology titled *Prabhat Sangeet* (1883).

It is well known how Rabindranath came to write his profoundly moving long poem "Nirjharer Swapnabhanga" in a fit of sudden illumination that had all the qualities of an epiphany. Sometime in 1881-82 Rabindranath lodged with his brother Jyotirindranath and Kadambari at 10 Sudder Street, Kolkata, just behind the National Museum. Here, as he later recalled in *Jibansmriti* (My Reminiscences): "One morning I happened to be standing on the verandah looking that way. The sun was just rising through the leafy tops of the trees. As I gazed, all of a sudden a lid seemed to fall from my eyes, and I found the world bathed in a wonderful radiance, with waves of beauty and joy swelling on every side. .... That very day the poem 'Nirjharer Swapnabhanga' (The Awakening of the Waterfall), gushed forth and coursed on like a cascade." Interestingly enough, Rabindranath's ecstatic exclamation *"jagiya uthechhe pran/ore uthali uthechhe bari/ore praner basana praner abeg rudhia rakhite nari"* [My aroused heart is overflowing with uncontrollable passion] was as sensual as it was spiritual, reminiscent of child Ramakrishna's *samadhi* at the sight of flying cranes in the cloudy sky or the sixteenth-century German reformer Martin Luther's wondrous vision of the merciful Christ upon reading St. Paul's letter to the Romans. The poem contains Tagore's paradigm of love and, as many critics agree, heralds the birth of Rabindranath, the future world poet. It is fairly certain that the inspiration behind this literary masterpiece was the poet's sister-in-law and that there developed an intimacy between the two young sensitive and impressionable individuals of almost the same age.

V It is noteworthy that the poet's later creations, *Kadi O Komal* (Sharps and Flats, 1886) and *Manasi,* in particular, brought in, to paraphrase his own observations, the fresh fruits of the heady autumn *(sharatkal)* in place of his former sentimental torrents of the rainy season *(barsakal).* However, the autumnal fruits also generated an ambivalent image of the female—at once passionate mistress and compassionate mother. Thus in his essay *Dui Bon* [Two Sisters], Tagore wrote that women are of two kinds: erotic *(priya)* and motherly *(ma).* To cite a few lines from the poem "Hriday Asan" (Heart's Throne) in *Kadi O Komal: Komal dukhani bahu sharame lataye/ Bikashita stan duti aguliya ray,/Tari majhkhane ki re rayechhe lukaye/Atishay-sayatan-gopan hriday!/Sei niralay sei komal asane/Duikhani snehasphuta staner chhayay/Kishor premer mridu pradoskirane/Anata ankhir tale rakhibe amay* [(Her) two tender arms cling shyly to cover and protect the two blossoming breasts./In between them lies hidden [her] carefully nurtured heart!/In that secret tender seat under the shade of the two loving breasts and her sunken eyes [she] will keep me ensconced at the faint twilight of youthful love]. In *Purna Milan* [Total Union], the poet's eroticism is acutely clear: *Trisita paran aji kandichhe katare/Tomare sarbanga diye karite darshan/Abar kothao—/Oi dehakhani buke tule neba bala/ Panchadash batsarer ek gachhi mala* [My thirsty heart is crying out/To behold you with my every limb./Girl, I shall place your body in my heart like a garland of fifteen.] Other pieces such as "Stan" (Breast), "Chumban" (Kiss), "Bibasana" (Undressed), "Bahu" (Arms), "Charan" (Feet), "Deher Milan" (Physical Union) etc. from *Kadi O Komal* celebrated the charms of the female physique.

In his maturer years Tagore came to view his relationship with women as something deeper and dearer than that of a partner in the game of love. In one of the poems of his *Sonar Tari,* the poet's *kabita kalpanalata* (Muse) or *manassundari* (the beautiful woman of imagination) becomes *jibaner adhisthatri debi* (presiding goddess of life) and *antaralakshmi* (goddess of the innermost recesses of heart). She also becomes what the poet calls *jibandebata* (lord of life). As he wrote in *Chitra* (1896): *Rate preyasir rup dhari/Tumi esechha praneswari,/Prate kakhan debir beshe/Tumi samukhe udile hese/Ami sambhrambhare rayechhi dandaye dure abanata shire/Aji nirmalbay shanta ushay nirjan naditire* [You came to me at night in the/Guise of a lover./At dawn you appeared smiling,/Decked as a Goddess./And awestruck, I remain standing on the desolate riverbank yonder/With my head hung low in wonder] ("Rate O Prabhate" [At Night and at Dawn]). For Tagore, thus, woman is *se yena tufan/yahare chanchal kare se tarike kare khan khan* (she is like a torrent./She pulverizes the boat she shakes); she is a *yadukari bachane chalane* (a charmer in her gait and speech), who is *prasadhan sadhane chatura* (an adept at making herself up), and yet the same woman lights and puts out a small lamp in her room./ After her morning bath she unlocks her hair and meditates her silent prayer *(grihakone chhoto deep jvalay nebay/ Snan sanga kari elochule prabhate nirab nibedane stab kare ekmane)* ("Ujjiban," *Mahua*).

This melange of opposite attitudes bears testimony to the poet's unstated albeit undoubted thesis that true human love is more than lust, it is also the channel of receiving the assurance of divine grace. The capstone for such a realization is to be noticed in *Mahua* (1928) which contains, among others, the following piece: "Woman is God's greatest gift descended on earth to bestow dignity and honour upon man" *[Nari se ye mahendrer dan,/esechhe dharitritale purusere sampite sanman,* "Spardha" (Audacity)]. In another piece the poet wrote: *Dibe se khuli/E ghor dhulir/Abaran./Tahar hate/ankhir pate/jagat-jaga jagaran./Se hasikhani anibe tani/sabar hasi/Gadibe geha, jagabe sneha/jibanrashi* [She will unveil/this dusty cloak./This world will awaken to her look./Her smile will make everyone smile,/ And nurture a home and evoke affection in every life] ("Shunya Hridayer Akankhya"[Desires of an Empty Heart]). Thus, as the poet proclaims in *Malini,* woman is neither a goddess nor an abstraction but a familiar female of flesh and blood—*debi na re, daya na re, gharer se meye.*

We also need to note that Rabindranath's idealized woman is no mere abstraction even though she is a product of his creative genius. Thus his *manasi* is a mix of sensuous experience as well as poetic imagination. As has been noted above, he did acknowledge *la femme* to be god's gift, and yet he could write: *Shudhu bidhatar sristi naha tumi nari./Purus gadechhe tore soundarya sanchari/Apan antar hate* [Woman, you're not created by god alone./You're also made of the beauty of man's heart]. In his famous lyric from *Manaspratima* [Idol of Imagination] he sang: *Tumi amara sadhera sadhana/Ami apana manera madhuri mishaye tomare karechhi rachana* [You're the prayers of my desire/ I've created you from my imagination of the sweet and the beautiful]. Thus the poet could announce to his *manasi* with confidence as well as humility: *Aj tumi apanake chinechha/Amar chena diye* [You now know who you are/By my reckoning].

In a number of subsequent poems, Rabindranath celebrated the beauty and beatitude of femininity in nature. His idea of *prem* has now been transmuted or sublimated into *bhalobasa* that is as much spiritual and cerebral *(manomai)* as it is passionate and physical. The poet even resurrects the Hindu cupid Madan, who suffered death by being immolated in Shiva's angry fire, as the deity of love reborn as a hero *(mrityu hate otho Pushpadhanu/Hey Atanu, birer tanute laha tanu).* Here we must recall Rabindranath's definition of *bhalobasa.* As early as 1881, the young poet had written in an essay in *Bharati* that "*bhalobasa* is more than mere self-surrender. Rather, it is surrendering the very best of one's self. *Bhalobasa* is not just installing the idol of the goddess in the heart. It is, more appropriately, installing the idol in the heart's sanctum." In his "Pashchim Yatrir Diary" (Diary of a Traveler to the West) written on board the vessel "Haruna Maru *en route* to South America in October 1924, Tagore expatiated on the meaning of *prem* in the double import of the word: *bhalolaga* (liking) and *bhalobasa* (love). The former is directed toward the self while the latter toward the other. *Bhalolaga* is gratified in enjoyment, *bhalobasa* achieves fulfillment in sacrifice and surrender. "*Bhalobasa* realizes itself in the spirit, it is the expansion of human personality," Tagore concluded.

In "Upahar" [Gift] Tagore wrote: *Bhule gechhi kabe tumi chhelebela ekdin/Maramer kachhe esechhile/Snehamay chhayamay sandhyasama ankhi meli/Ekbar bujhi hesechhile/ Age ke janita balo kata ki lukano chhila/Hriday nibhrite/ tomar nayan diya amar nijer hiya/Painu dekhite* [I have forgotten when in my youth you came to my heart/And looked at me with your loving eyes cool as the evening shadows./Who could have known what treasure was hidden in my heart until I could discover it through your gaze] *(Sandhyasangit).* The poet's lover is not just an erotic playmate of youth; she is also his soulmate in life and beyond. His idea of femininity shows a remarkable fusion of Western and Eastern ideas in his reconstruction of the character of Chitrangada in the Hindu epic *Mahabharata.* As he makes her proclaim in the famous lyrical play *Chitrangada: Ami Chitrangada ami rajendranandini/Debi nahi, nahi samanya ramani./Puja kari rakhibe mathay, seo ami/Nai; abahela kari pusiya rakhibe/ Pichhe, seo ami nahi. Yadi parshve rakho/More sankater pathe, duruha chintar/Yadi angsha dao, yadi anumati karo/Kathin brater taba sahay haite,/Yadi sukhe duhkhe more karo sahachari,/Amar paibe tabe parichay.* [I am princess Chitrangada,/Not a goddess to be worshiped/On an altar,/Nor a mere woman pushed behind/With indifference./If you let me walk beside you/In weal and woe/And make me your comrade/ In difficult venture,/You will know me/For what I am.] "In her," observes Rajat Ray, "the older Indian idea of wife as a partner in the duties of family life *(sahadharmini)* had developed, under Western influence, into the romantic concept of a comrade in perilous action." Clinton Seely further clarifies the term *bhalobasa* by comparing it to the commonly understood terms such as sneha (a kind of filial attraction) and *prem* (amorous romantic love). *Bhalobasa,* Seely concludes, "comprehends both *sneha* and *prem."* Niharranjan Ray astutely observes that for Tagore "love cannot deny or bypass the reality of the body's desire; but a love which never learns to go beyond the body knows no real fulfillment, no peace, and is, therefore, unreal." Indeed, as the poet himself has written in *Creative Unity,* "in human nature sexual passion is fiercely individual and destructive, but dominated by the ideal of love, it has been made to flower into a perfection of beauty, becoming in its best expression symbolical of the spiritual truth in man which is his kinship of love with the Infinite." In his poem "Nisphal Kamana" [Unrequited Passion] he had admonished: *Bhalobaso, preme hao bali,/Cheona tahare./Akankhar dhan nahe atma manaber/* [Love (her), and be strong in love,/but do not desire her./Human soul is not an object of lust.]

Rabindranath has often been seen as a mystic for whom, in Vaishnavic terms, *atmendriya pritiichha* [self-centered love and desire] or *eros* [*kam*] coalesced in love for God [*prem*], krishnendriya pritiichha [Krishna—or God-centered love and desire]. In other words, the poet's idea of love is tantalizingly comparable to the Christian idea of *agape.* However, I argue that Rabindranath's idea of love cannot be apprehended by regarding him a mystic or regarding his idea of *prem* or *eros* as divine *agape.* Abbé Henri Bremond distinguishes between mystical, that is, religious and poetical activity and considers the latter as an imperfect form of the former. Even if poetry is considered as a kind of prayer in that it employs "some of the resources of the deep-seated soul," it is, according to Bremond, an imitation of mystical prayer, an *ersatz* religious solution to soteriological problems.

Then, *agape* is radically different from *eros. Agape* is a noble spiritual love that mimics the love of God for all His creations. In *agape,* all things are loved unconditionally with no consideration of a transactional *quid pro quo.* It is unmotivated or as the Bengali expression has it *ahaituki prem. Eros,* on the other hand, is motivated by the acquisition of happiness. Eros recognizes value in the object of love and loves it. *Agape* loves and creates value in its object of love. As the psychologist Erich Fromm has it, eros is based on the proposition "I love you because I need you" while *agape* is predicated on the plea "I need you because I love you." *Eros* is man's way to God, *agape* is God's way to man.

Jagadish Bhattacharya posits, following the definition of the seventeenth-century Bengali aesthetician Kabikarnapura, that Rabindranath's idea of love could be something analogous to suprasensuous eros or *pritirati,* that is a feeling or sentiment which delights *(rati)* the heart but remains *asamproyagabisaya* or devoid of carnality. Rabindranath's idea of *pritirati,* is poignantly expressed in his poem *Banaspati* (The *Dendron*) in which, standing in the sunset hours of life, the tired titan expressed his desire for a final repose and quiet after having struggled with the *Sturm und Drang* of his soul buffeted by the crosscurrents of his unrequited passion and unfulfilled mission in life. In his response of December 28, 1924 to the overture of his Argentine hostess, who had written him to say "I have gone through such joy and such sufferings all these days! Joy because I felt near you; sufferings, because you ignored my nearness," the aging and ailing Rabindranath wrote to that "incomparable one" *[tulanahinare]* he had met "on the verdant bank of the blue ocean" *[sunil sagarer shyamal kinare]: Daya karo, daya karo, aranyak ei tapaswire,/ Dhairya dharo, ogo digangana,/Byartha karibare tay ashanta abege phire phire/baner angane matiyo na./E ki tibra prem, e ye shilabristi nirmam duhsaha—/Duranta chumban-bege taba/Chhindite jharate chao andha sukhe, kaha more kaha,/kishor korak naba naba?/Asuk tomar prem diptirupe nilambartale,/Shaktirupe eso, digangana./Uthuk spandita hoye sakhe sakhe pallabe balkale/Sughambhir tomar bandana./Dao tare sei tej mahatwe yahar samadhan,/Sarthak hok se banaspati./Biswer anjali yena bhariya karite pare dan/Tapsyar purna parinati.* [Hold back, please, O Goddess of Directions, do not distract this mendicant of the forest with your restless desire./ The hailstorm of your intense passion is merciless and unbearable./ Tell me, do you intend to pluck the new born buds with your violent kisses?/ Let your love descend as the light from the blue sky/ And you, Goddess, come as the primal energy, *Shakti.*/Let the leaves and the bark of this *dendron* pulsate in singing your paean./ Endow it with your power so that it may achieve the final consummation of its prayers by offering all it has to the world at large].

Especially Tagore's last three collections of poems—*Rogshayyay* (In Sickbed), *Arogya,* (Recovery), and *Janmadine* (On My Birthday) written during October 1940-March 1941—reveal an enigmatic convergence of the artist and the ascetic. All the pieces of these collections are characterized by a quiet grandeur: *shanta rasa.* Though, according to Bagbhatta, this particular rasa or aesthetic delight has its marker in *samyakjnan,* that is, awareness of the Absolute Soul *(Paramatman)* or God, in Tagore *shanta rasa* displays the unity of the two divergent consciousness: "the sweet earthy passion" *(martyer madhuratama asakti)* and "the sublime freedom of the heavens" *(akasher nirmalatama mukti).* This consciousness informs his idea of love or *bhalobasa* as it evolved from the impetuous, rebellious, and "delirious cascading waterfall" *(nirjharer pralapkallol)* of his youth to a serene and silent prayer "in cosmic quiescence" *(nikhiler brihat shantite).* In the sunset hours of his life, in a relatively obscure but a truly lyrical piece titled "Sandhyay" [In the Evening], the poet beseeches his beloved to be as beautiful, serene, and quiet as the evening and asks her to come to his life all by herself: *Ogo tumi sandhyar mata hao ...omni sundar shanta ...mata dhire dhire amar jibantire/Barek dandao ekakini.*

Rabindranath was a humanist *par excellence* who loved this beautiful earth and its colorful inhabitants so much that he refused to depart from this world: "I do not want to die in this beautiful world,/ But live in the hearts of men" *[Marite chahina ami, sundar bhubane, /manaber majhe ami banchibare chai] (Kadi O Komal).* He candidly confessed to his commitments to the world at large in his letter to his Argentine hostess and admirer Victoria Ocampo: "My true home is there where from my surroundings comes the call to me to bring out the best that I have, for that inevitably leads me to the touch with the universal." He wrote in his Reminiscences: "I guess my work has only one theme—reconciling the finite with the infinite."

Tagore's quintessential humanism is implicit in his concepts of *dharma* and *debata.* For him *dharma,* loosely translated as religion, is *Manuser Dharma* (Religion of Man, 1931) and *debata* (God) is *Jibandebata* (Lord of Life). As he explained: "That creative energy inside me which is unifying as well as signifying all the pleasures and pain of my life, and my changing self through many rebirths I had called Lord of Life *(Jibandebata).*" The *Jibandebata* is also, as Tagore himself has said borrowing the *Baul* (rustic roving singing minstrels) imagery, "the man or woman of the heart" or *maner manus.* A noteworthy feature of Tagore's God is that He presides over His created world. Tagore has little patience with Shankaracharya's *mayavad* that reduces this world to a mere illusion or a dream. To him, this world, created by God, is intensely real. "Without the world," he declares, "God would be phantasm, without God the world would be chaos." Tagore's conviction that "to know the Supreme Joy through all earthly love, to perceive the visible form of the Exquisite One through the world of beauty is what I call the realisation of freedom" is a telling testament of his pronounced earth-credo or terraphilia.

As early as 1901 Rabindranath wrote: *Bairagya sadhane mukti, se amar nai/Asankhya bandhan-majhe mahanandamai/ Labhiba muktir swad* [Deliverance is not for me in renunciation. /I feel the embrace of freedom in a thousand bonds of delight]. About three decades later, he reiterated: *Shudhayo na more tumi mukti kotha, mukti kare kai,/Ami sadhak nai, ami guru nai/Ami kabi, achhi/Dharanir ati kachhakachhi/Eparer kheyar ghatay* [Ask me not what salvation means or where to get it./ Sage or mentor I'm not./I am but a poet who stays close to this earth on this side of the bank (of life)]. In another poem, he confessed: "How I wish to quench my thirst by drinking time and again the wine of bliss from all the vessels of this world" *[Ichha kare barbar mitaite sadh/Pan kari biswer sakal patra hate/Anandamadiradhara naba naba srote].* Sometime later, the poet announced: *Labhiachhi jibaloke manbjanmer adhikar,/ Dhanya ei soubhagya amar* [I'm blessed to be born a human in this world living beings] ("Barsashes" [Year End], 1926). In a short poem composed toward the end of his life the poet proclaimed in no uncertain terms: *Shes sparsa niye yaba yabe dharanir bale yabo, 'Tomar dhulir tilak parechhi bhale; dekhechhi nityer jyoti duryoger mayar adale./Satyer anandarup e dhulite niyechhe murati/Ei jene e dhulay rakhinu pranati* [When I go having touched this earth for the last time, I would say, 'Today I have marked my forehead with your dust;/I have seen the bright eternity behind the mist of danger and turmoil./ I know that the beautiful truth has realized itself and I place my head on the dust (of this world)']. He had sung: *Amar mukti alloy alloy ei akashe/Amar mukti dhulay dhulay ghase ghase/ Amar mukti sarbajaner maner majheDuhkha-bipad tuchha kara kathin kaje* [My deliverance is in the lighted firmament, in every dust particle and in every grass of the earth/ ... My salvation is in the universal mind and in my exertions defying all dangers and disappointments]. The ailing *Bisvakabi* [World Poet] tendered his final offering not to a deity of the distant heavens but to humanity of this world: *Ami bratya, ami mantrahin./Sakal mandirer bahire amar puja aj samapta hala/ Deblok theke/Manabloke,/Akashe jyotirmay puruse/Ar maner manuse amar antartama anande* [I am the uninitiated pariah,/ Today I have performed my final worship with profound bliss of the bright God of the skies/And the Man of My Heart on this world away from the temples] (*Patraput* [The Leaves], 1936).

Yet Tagore was far from a naïve starry-eyed philanthropist or a supramundane mystic or prophet. Even though he delighted in his interaction with peoples and ideas, he was also painfully aware of the deceit, deviousness, and iniquity of his world. Some of his contemporaries considered him as a poet of ethereal, even unreal *[bastutantrahin]* fantasies. A one-time friend of the poet, Narendranath Datta (premonastic name of Swami Vivekananda, 1863-1902), who had taken lessons in Brahmo prayer songs from Rabindranath, called him a purveyor of "erotic venom." An influential poet and literary critic in Britian ridiculed Tagore's English translation of his own poems as the product of an illiterate Indian. On October 25, 1930 he wrote to Indira: "By god's grace I was born with a tough physique so that I could take as much abuse as I can from my own country[men]." On September 14, 1933 Rabindranath wrote: "It is a matter of great regret that for [some people] scandal mongering makes a good living. I thus realize how widespread and deep is the animus against me in my country. How little pain my country people feel by hurting and insulting me! Had this not been the case, scurrilous criticisms against me would not have been so profitable." Tagore's biographer Mukhopadhyay laments: "At what an inauspicious moment did he compose *Sonar Tari!* No other single creation of Rabindranath spewed so much flattery as well as vitriol either earlier or later....Really speaking, the poet was actually the target of attack, his poetry an excuse, because some people sought to belittle those qualities of Rabindranath's multifaceted genius that had been recognized by the majority of the intellectuals of the country."

Although Tagore frankly confessed to being a romantic he did reckon with his personal struggle against the terrifying real world on his own terms. He would deal with it by bringing together the *bhairab* [terrifying reality] and the *sundar* [the ideal and the beautiful]. He wrote: *Yetha oi bastab jagat/ Sekhane anagonar path/Achhe amar chena./Sethakar dena/ Shodh kari—se nahe kathai taha jani/ tahar ahban ami mani./ Shoukhin bastab setha nahi hai./Sethay sundar yena bhairaber sathe/Chale hate hate* [I'm familiar with the road to the real world./I know, too, that I can't pay my debts to it in words/But I respond to its call./...No fancy reality could be found there./ There the terrific and the terrible walk hand in hand./] His *Sheslekha,* composed in the last year of his life contain a couple of poems that reveal his personal struggle: *Rupnaraner kule/Jege uthilam,/Janilam e jagat svapna nai./Rakter akashe dekhilam/Apanar rup,/Chinilam apanare aghate aghate/bedanay bedanay;/Satya ye kathin,/Kathinere bhalobasilam,/Se kakhano kare na banchana./Amrityur duhkher tapasya e jiban,/Satyer darun mulya labh karibare,/Mirtyute sakal dena shodh kare dite* [I awoke on the bank of the Rupnaran/And realized that this world is not a phantasm./I beheld my visage etched in blood,/And recognized myself amidst many hurts and aches;/I fell in love with the relentless reality that knows no deception./This life of mine is a long painful prayer till I redeem all my debts and receive the terrible price of truth in death].

The very last piece, dictated from deathbed is eloquent, elegant, and evocative: *Tomar sristir path rekhechha akirna kari/Bichitra chhalanajale/He chhalanamayi./Mithya bisvasher phand petechha nipun hate/Saral jibane./Ei prabanchanadiye mahatvere karechha chinhita./...Satyere se pai/Apan aloke—dhouta antare antare./Kichhute parena tare prabanchite,/Shes puraskar niye yai se ye/Apan bhandare./Anayase ye perechhe chhalana sahite/Se pay tomar hate/Shantir akshay adhikar* [Sorceress, you've strewn the path of/Your creation in a mesh of varied wiles./Cleverly you've laid a snare of false beliefs/In artless lives./You've marked the (honest) and great with deceptions/....Though crooked outside/He's upright within,/And that is his pride./Though all call him disturbed,/He finds truth in the inner recesses of his heart/Washed clean by his inner light./Nothing can fool him;/He carries to his treasure-house/His final reward./He who could put up with your deceit receives from you the right/To everlasting peace].

Tagore's humanism in its cosmic expanse makes him an aesthete whose experience of beauty and the creative art expressed in it go against the grain of ancient Indian or Vedantic aesthetics which, to quote a sentence from a modern exponent of the subject, "makes us progressively conscious of the illusoriness of the empirical world and ego-life and of the reality of the higher and non-attached spirit within us." However, Tagore did not think that the function of art was to make us realize "the illusoriness of the empirical world" and the hyper-reality of a higher world. By detachment and disinterestedness of aesthetic experience he understood detachment from the exigencies of action and never from the world of humanity and of nature where his every step on the green meadow or in the grove has filled his life with enchanting and exciting delight *(Ghase ghase pa phelechhi baner pathe jete/phuler gandhe bharechhe man uthechhe pran mete).* As he wrote, "from the dawn of history the poets and artists have been infusing the colours and music of their own soul into the structure of existence. And from this I have known certainly that the earth and the sky are woven with the fibres of man's mind." He has thus found his niche under the starry firmament and his song springs forth in utter amazement *(Akash-bhara surya-tara,/ Bishwa-bhara pran/Tahari majhkhane ami peyechhi, peyechhi mor sthan./Bismaye jage, jage amar pran).* One of the most poignant pieces proclaiming the poet's aesthetic amalgam of human and cosmic love may be found in the collection titled *Chaitali* [Late Harvest] (1896): *Amader dujaner pratham chumban./Ananta nakshatralok uthila shihari/ Amader chakshe ela ashrujal bhari* (Our first kiss./The limitless galaxy shuddered./ Tears filled our eyes). This is what Theodor Lipps had called *Einfühlung* or empathy. This empathy is love in all its forms: love between a man and a woman *(eros),* man's love for God and God's for man *(agape),* and aesthetic love *(Einfühlung),* that is, love for the world at large through empathy, which means "feeling into" rather than sympathy, which means "feeling with."

We should bear in mind that the poet had expressed such sentiments eloquently earlier in his poem "Ananta Prem" [Love Eternal]: *Nikhiler shukh nikhiler dukh/Nikhil praner priti/ Ekti premer majhare mishechhe/ sakal premer smriti/Sakal kaler sakal premer giti* [The bliss, blight, and love of the world has merged into one love that holds the memory and music of universal love for all times]. Elsewhere he endorsed the sentiment of a woman poet of medieval India and cited her in his own translation: I salute the Life in the house and the Life abroad in the unknown,/The Life full of joy and the Life weary with its pains,/The Life eternally moving, rocking the world into stillness,/The Life deep and silent, breaking out into roaring waves. Nirad Chaudhuri observes that mystical faith in "Rabindranath Tagore's philosophy of life is at once rooted in the faith in earthly existence and in life beyond death." In other words, following Abu Sayeed Ayyub, it may be concluded that for Rabindranath love of woman, nature, and god is a connected concept.

The lover Rabindranath cannot be separated from the aesthetic priest, the worshiper of his *Jibandebata.* As he had declared in a lecture in the United States in 1917: "With the growth of man's spiritual life, our worship has become worship of love." This worship is also accompanied with a gender transformation of the object of love. Thus the poet's ususal lover, the woman, now becomes a male with a masculine name *Jibandebata, antaratama* (the most intimate one) to whom the male poet now expresses his love as a woman (in Edward Thompson's unkind words expressing a "zenana imagery"): *Ohe anaratama,/mitechhe ki taba sakal tiyas/Asi antare mama?/Duhkhasukher laksa dharay/Patra bharia diyachhi tomay,/Nithur pidane ningadi baksa/Dalita draksa sama./* [My lord, have you drunk enough of me? /I have crushed my breast like vineyards,/ filling your cup with my joys and sorrows/].

This reversal of gender whereby the poet himself becomes a woman supplicating to a male lover must have been facilitated by his Vaishnabic cultural heritage. Interestingly enough, Rabindranath's poetic career began as the precocious Bhanusingha composing erotic lyrics on the Vaishnavic theme of the love between Radha and Krishna. In his advancing years, especially past his middle age, the poet harked back to the same font of his poetic consciousness, the Vaishnava devotional style of feminization of the male devotee. Thus the poems addressed to his *Jibandebata* are more philosophical versions of his romantic lyrics of adolescence and early youth transforming his erotic consciousness into *prem* (in the true sense of *bhalobasa*): *Sab cheye satya mor, sei mrityunjay,/se amar prem./Tare ami rakhiya elem/Aparibartan arghya tomar uddeshe* [My love is immortal and it's the highest truth (of my life)./That eternal offering of mine I have dedicated to you].

The unabashed romantic matured into a brooding philosopher who combined in himself the *premik* (lover) and the *pujari* (worshiper). This erotic ascetic, the dendron of the forest *(aranyak banaspati)*, awaited till his dying day, staking all his possessions, the advent of his surreal lover, *Jibandebata,* the darling deity of life, who is also *kautukmayi antaryami* (playful indwelling woman), *antartama jibannath* (lord of life who is inside the innermost), or *priyatama pranesh* (the most beloved lord of life): For the return of the One/ Who has left me on the road,/ I eagerly wait with all my load. / He is never seen but he can see,/ Yet thus unseen he loves me. /My heart is lost in my secret affair/ With that amazing intimate Lover *(Amar sakal niye base achhi/ Sarbanasher ashay /Ami tar lagi path cheye achhi/ Pathe ye jan bhasay/ Ye jan dey na dekha yay ye dekhe/ Bhalobase adal theke/Amar man majechhe sei gabhirer/ Gopan bhalobasay).*

Rabindranath Tagore was no world-weary self-abnegating ascetic. He was a seeker of the ultimate freedom and beauty in this life on this planet, and not a beyonder. "Not self-immolation, but self-expression must be our aim," the poet proclaimed—and this should serve as his enduring epitaph.

The Parrot's Tale

Rabindranath Tagore

— 1 —

Once there was a bird. It was an utterly foolish bird. It sang songs, but did not read the scriptures. It flew, it jumped, but did not have the faintest sense of etiquette.

The King said, "Such birds! They are of no use at all. They only eat the fruits in the orchards and the royal fruit-market runs a deficit."

He called the minister, and commanded, "Educate it."

— 2 —

The King's nephew was given the responsibility of educating the bird.

The scholars held long discussions, the subject being — "What is the reason behind the foolishness of this creature?"

The conclusion was: much learning could not be stored in the tiny nest that the bird could make with just chips and twigs. So, first of all, it was necessary to build a good cage for it.

The scholars got amply rewarded and went home merrily.

— 3 —

The goldsmith started building the cage. The cage turned out to be so exquisite that everyone under the sun rushed to see it. Some said, "Education indeed!" Others said, "Education or no education, at least the bird has got the cage! What a lucky bird!"

The goldsmith got a bagful of rewards. He set out for home cheerfully.

The pundit came to teach the bird. He took a pinch of snuff and said, "A few books won't do."

The nephew summoned the scribes. They copied from the books and copied from those copies and made an enormous mound of such things. Whoever saw it, said, "Bravo! Learning is going to overflow!"

The scribes got cartfuls of rewards. At once they rushed home. None of their descendants faced any poverty ever since.

The nephew was always busy, doing endless number of things regarding the surveillance of the precious cage. Repairs were quite frequent. Apart from that, there was the washing and the cleaning and the polishing of the cage. Everyone admitted, "Sure signs of improvement."

Many people were employed and to supervise them, many more people were employed. Each of them got a handful of coins every month and filled their chests with them.

They, their brothers, sisters and cousins began to live in great luxury and happiness.

— 4 —

The world lacks many things; only fault-finders are there in plenty. They said, "There are improvements of the cage all right, but nobody cares for the bird."

The words reached the King's ears. He called the nephew and said, "What's this I hear, dear nephew?"

The nephew said, "Your Majesty! If you want to know the truth then call the goldsmith, send for the pundits and the scribes, summon the repairmen and their supervisors. The fault-finders cannot make both ends meet and talk nonsense."

The situation became crystal-clear to the King, and a gold necklace adorned the nephew's neck.

— 5 —

The King wished to see for himself the lightening speed at which education was proceeding. So one day he came to the education center with his entire entourage of friends, companions and courtiers.

As soon as he reached the entrance, there arose a chorus of bells and drums and harps and flutes and lyres and lutes and cellos and violins and cymbals and mandolins and trombones and bassoons and harpsichords and clavichords. The pundits swung their pig-tails and started chanting hymns at the top of their voices. The repairmen and the laborers and the goldsmith and the scribes and the supervisors and the cousins greeted the King with a huge uproar.

The Nephew said, "Your Majesty! What do you think?"

The King said, "Amazing! This is a non-trivial amount of sound!"

The Nephew said, "It's not just the sound Your Majesty, there is also a non-trivial amount of money behind it."

The King was extremely pleased. He started back. He came out of the front door and was about to ride his elephant, when a fault-finder, who had been hiding in a bush, yelled, "Your Majesty! Have you looked at the bird?"

The King was startled. He said, "Oh! I forgot. I didn't see the bird after all."

He went in once again and told the pundit, "I want to see your method of educating the bird."

And he saw it. Very pleasing indeed. The method was so overwhelming compared to the bird that one could hardly notice the bird. It seemed it was rather irrelevant to look at the bird. The King understood that the arrangements were faultless. There was no corn in the cage, no water either. Only heaps of pages had been torn out from heaps of books; and with the tip of a pen, those pages were being stuffed into the bird's mouth. There was no room in the mouth for the bird to squeeze out a cry, let alone a tune. It was really a terribly pleasing sight.

This time, before mounting the elephant, the King ordered the ear-pulling expert to pull the fault-finder's ears severely.

— 6 —

In a rather respectable and predictable way, the bird became half-dead as the days passed. The guardians understood that the situation was hopeful. But still — as its bad habits were — the bird looked at the morning sun and flapped its wings in a very objectionable manner. Some days it was even found to make an attempt to break the rods of the cage with its sickly beak.

The administrator said, "What audacity!"

Immediately, the blacksmith came to the education department with bellows and fire and hammer and chisels. His hits were absolutely spectacular! An iron chain was manufactured and the wings of the bird were cut off. The King's relatives shook their heads gravely and said, "In this land, you see, the birds are not only stupid, but ungrateful as well."

Then the pundits came with a pen in one hand and a spear in another and did something which one could really call education.

The blacksmith became very well-to-do. His wife got gold ornaments. The administrator gained a title from the King for his alertness.

— 7 —

The bird died — no one knew when. The infamous fault-finder spread the news, "The bird has died."

The King called the nephew and asked, "Dear nephew, what is this that I hear?"

The nephew said, "Your Majesty, the bird's education is now complete."

The King asked, "Does it still jump?"

The nephew said, "God forbid."

"Does it still fly?"

"No."

"Does it sing any more?"

"No."

"Does it scream if it doesn't get food?"

"No."

The King said, "Bring the bird in. I would like to see it."

The bird was brought in. With it came the administrator, the guards, the horsemen. The King felt the bird. It didn't open its mouth and didn't utter a word. Only the pages of books, stuffed inside its stomach, raised a ruffling sound.

Outside, where the gentle south wind and the blossoming woods were heralding spring, the young green leaves filled the sky with a deep and heavy sigh.

Rabindranath and World-Life

(Rabindranath O Bishwajiban)

Niharranjan Ray

The two poems of Rabindranath, "Antaryami" (The Interiorized One) and "Jibandebata" (Lord of Life) in the collection titled *Chitra* reveal a delectable mystery of the poet's life.

E ki kautuk nityanutan
Ogo kautukmayi
Ami yaha kicchu chahi balibare

Balite diteccha kai?
Antar majhe basi aharaha
Mukh hote tumi bhasa kade laha
Mor katha laye tumi katha kaha
Mishaye apan surey
Ki balite chai sab bhule yai
Tumi ya balao ami bali tai
Sangitsrote kul nahi pai
Kotha bhese yai dure.
("Antaryami", *Chitra*)

[What's this whimsy of yours
My capricious one!
Why don't you let me say my bit?
Seated inside me all the time
You speak stealing my word
And I forget mine and speak
Only what you wish me to.
I am being swept away by the
Surging waves of my lyrics.]

Who is this capricious and mysterious female commandeering the poet's thoughts into his lyrics and poems? He has no control over his own words—all his output happens to be the product of this amazing *dea ludens* (lit. "playful goddess," *rahasyamayi kautukmayi*)?

Ohe antaratama
Mitechhe ki taba sakal tiyas
Asi antare mama?
Duhkha sukher laksa dharay
Patra bhariya diyechhi tomay
Nithur pidane ningadi baksa
Dalita draksa sama
("Jibandebata", *ibid*)

[My lord, have you drunk enough of me?

I have crushed my breast like vineyards,
Filling your cup with my joys and sorrows.]

Who is this *antaratama*, the innermost one to whom he offers cupful of his weal and woes wrung out of his heart? The poet has declared her as the one who resides in his innermost being—the presiding deity of his life, *Jibandebata* [note the change of gender here. Translator] He hasn't sought him out. The *jibandebata* has welcomed him. This god (or goddess) is the guardian angel whom the poet offers his lyrics and poems as ritual flowers.

The poet's life is a lyre, as it were, tuned by *Jibandebata*, who makes the poet create music. Does this deity reside in the poet's own imagination, who bursts out of his heart in poetic form? Probably his own thoughts, sensation, or consciousness, or realization (*anubhuti*) have become the sovereign lord of his whole life to whom the humble poet brings his meager offerings:

Debi, nishidin kari paranpan
Charane ditechhi ani
Mor jibaner sakal srestha sadher dhan,
Byartha sadhan khani.
...Tumi yadi debi palace kebal
Kara kataksha sneha sukomal
Ekti bindu phela yadi ankhi jal
Karuna mani.
Sab hate tabe sarthak habe
Byartha sadhan khani. (ibid)
[...My goddess, I bring to your feet
All my failed enterprise,
The prized possession of my life.
...I shall deem it very kind of you
If you, Debi, look at me
With compassion even for a moment.
Then all my failed efforts
Will have received some justification.]

There is little doubt that this deity is the poet's *Jibandebata.* All his failings and failures, his unspoken words, unsung lyrics, and unfulfilled aspirations have been offered to this deity's feet seeking fulfillment. But, who's this god?

All human beings harbour a creative impulse inside them propelling them to express themselves in art and literature, indeed in all their actions. Rabindranath often felt the presence of this creative impulse deeply. An intense urge from within him expressed itself through his work. The three pieces cited above illustrate how this *anubhuti* manifests itself aesthetically. This impulse from within him triggers his works to express it.

But the question is: Does this CREATIVE IMPULSE well up from within only? Isn't there an external source for it? Does this impulse, which Rabindranath calls *kautukmayi antaryami* [the mysterious indwelling deity], awaken spontaneously without any external stimuli? I think not, though I cannot argue my point philosophically. Human mind appears to be incapable of appreciating the beauty of the world unless it is inspired by something in this world or universal life *(vishwajiban)* that triggers human capacity to appreciate beauty. Human creativity is thus dependent upon forces from the phenomenal world outside. Surely Tagore's creative impulse was triggered by the wonderful expression of the variegated life of the world at large.

Human creative impulse, then, does have a springboard and its *anubhuti* is the lord of life or *Jibaner Adhishwar*, that is *Jibandebata.* Thus Tagore's poetic *oeuvres* owe to this intimate deity. He feels that all his creations owe to this impulse's grace. He has offered cupfuls of his joys and sorrows and his life's greatest treasure to its feet, as it were, and sought assurance that his innermost one [*antaratma*] is gratified by them. This poet calls this impulse the mysterious innermost being [*kautukmayi antaryami*] who has filled the poet's life with new ventures and surprises at all times. As this impulse gains stature inside the poet, he becomes its puppet and devotee, as could be seen in a few poems of *Chitra.*

However, I do not certainly claim that his empathy with the cosmic life or universal life (*bishwajiban*) and his creative impulse are one and the same thing. I mean to posit that Tagore's awareness of this expansive life since his early youth fueled the creative impulse for his work. This awareness has found unique expression at different stages of his life; its flow has taken twists and turns at times—waning in winter and waxing in the rainy season. I claim, even at the risk of repeating myself, that the poet's creative impulse is instigated by his awareness of the cosmic life and this awareness has been identified by him later as his lord of life.

We get the first clear hint of this awareness in some of Tagore's letters and in his reminiscences. All of us are familiar with his experience of this sensation as he stood on the balcony of the Sudder Street residence looking at the garden at the eastern corner of the street. We may very well skip this episode, but two passages from the poet's letters merit mention. In one of his letters the poet wrote:

My memory of my childhood is hazy, though I distinctly recall how some mornings I suddenly felt an intense joy of life (*Jibanananda*) apparently for no reasons whatsoever. All quarters of the world seemed to be enveloped in mystery. In the granary I used to dig the soil with a stick eager to discover something unknown. I enjoyed the company of a half-familiar gigantic being formed in different shapes out of the beauty and smell, and movements of the earth, the coconut trees in the compound of my home, the banyan tree on the bank of the pond, the shadows upon its waters, the noise from the street, the call of the kite, and the aroma from the garden.

Part of another letter reads:

We can derive great happiness from nature by feeling an intimate connection with it. Our pulse beats along with the grass, the breeze, the revolving light and shadow, the movement of the planets and stars, and the innumerable successions of life on earth. We are set in the same rhythm with the world and our mind responds to its movement and music....We are not a class apart from what we call inanimate and thus we coexist, otherwise there would been two distinct worlds.

Although most poets have enjoyed a deep delight in nature, in Rabindranath this bliss has found a special intensity. He has felt a profound intimacy (*nigudha atmiyata*) with nature's abundant expressions. All the beautiful and variegated expressions of the world of nature filled his being with a single grand whole....The sensation of this mysterious innermost one suddenly touches the poet's soul making it restive and frantic apparently for no reason. The world of nature vibrating within the poet's heart leads it to seek itself out in the outer world. It's not easy to recognize this *anubhuti*, it's a mysterious, mystical, quasi-familiar being. Perhaps this wondrous mystery is hidden in every expression of nature. The truth, however, is that it actually lies within the poet's psyche and not elsewhere. Yet there is little doubt that this stranger resides in the poet's interiority as his indwelling companion—the first faint signifier of cosmic life. This faint hint becomes clearer and expresses itself beautifully for the first time in numerous poems of *Prbhatsangit* [Song of the Dawn], especially "Nirjharer Swapnabhanga" [The Spring Wakes from Its Dreams]. The sentiment and sensation welling up to burst out of the poet's *soma* and psyche (*deha-mon*) find their release in the infinite varieties of the phenomenal world....

Hriday aji mor kemane gela khuli
Jagat asi setha karichhe kolakuli.
Dharay ache yata manus shata shata
Asichhe prane mor hasichhe galagali
... ...
Paran pure gela harase hala bhor
Jagate keha nai, sabai prane mor.
[My heart unfolded today
To embrace the world.
All the humanity of this earth
Have come to join my life.
... ...
My life has filled with joy and when dawn came
Every one in the world has come in my life.]

Or,

Aji e prabhate rabir kar
Kemane pashila praner par
Kemane pashila guhar andhare,
Prabhat pakhir gan.
Na jani kenare etadin pare
Jagiya uthila pran.
("Nirjharer Swapnabhanga", *Prabhat-Sangeet.*)

[How have the sun's rays in my heart
Entered this morning! How have the songs
Of morning birds into the dark cave broken!
Who knows why, after long, my soul has woken!]

Everywhere one notes occasional flashes of this sensation. The poet subsequently named it *Jibandebata* [lord of life] and this *anubhuti*, appearing in various guises, has been his intimate consort throughout his life. Nevertheless, in *Prabhatsangit* this sensation is still pretty vague and unformed.

It is not really difficult to discern the concept of this sensation and it is Rabindranath's favourite and familiar concept. In fact the poet himself has explained the concept behind his *anubhuti* in numerous poetical works and other writings. It also has been echoed by some thinkers in our country and overseas. The innumerable visible manifestations of universal life could be realized within the confines of our heart as a complete sensation [*anubhuti*]. However, this *akhanda anubhuti* [undivided sensation] refuses to rest within, always seeking to break all bounds to realize itself in the infinite universal life. To be sure, what is limitless is neither real nor realizable; the unbound is formless, it has its *raison d'etre* only with bounds. The unlimited cannot be realized unless it is comprehended within limits. By the same token, nothing within bounds can reach perfection until it transcends its limitedness and merges in the unlimited and the unformed. The finite and the infinite, the form and the formless, the part and the whole coexist. Our individual mortal life is thus organically related to the universal eternal life. We realize the latter within the finitude of our personal life. There is nothing in creation that cannot be apprehended in our interiorized feelings. Otherwise, our individual life, even the life universal, would be devoid of any meaning.

A poem composed in his maturer years expresses this concept wonderfully:

Dhup apanare milaite chahe gandhe
Gandha se chahe dhupere rahite jude
Sur apanare yog dite chahe chhande
Chhanda apani phire yete chai sure.
Bhab pete chai ruper majhare anga
Rup pate chai bhaber majhare chhada
Asim se chahe simar nibid sanga
Sima hate chai asimer majhe hara.
Pralay srijabe na jani e kar yukti
Bhab hate rupe abiram yawa asa
Bandha phirichhe khunjiya apan mukti
Mukti magichhe bandhaner majhe basa.
(*Chhabi O Gan.*)

[The incense wants to dissolve into its aroma
And the aroma wants to stick to the incense
The music wants to join the meter
The meter wants to return to the tune.
The thoughts seek form and
Form seeks release in thoughts.
The infinite seeks close touch of the finite
The finite wants to be lost in the infinite.
Whose idea is this: creation and dissolution?
Moving back and forth from thought to form?
Confinement seeking release and freedom residing in restraint?]

....As will be seen later, as the poet advanced in age, his realization of an intimate connection with the cosmic life grew deeper and possessed his literary life. While his *Prabhatsangit* gives a faint hint to this realization, it becomes clearer in

"Rahur Prem" [The Demon's Love] (*Chhabi O Gan*) [Pictures and Songs]:

Shunechhi amare bhala lage na
Nai ba lagila tor,
Kathin bandhane charan bediya
Chirakal tore raba ankadiya
Lauha shrinkhaler dor.
Tui ta amar sangi abhagini,
Bandhiachhi karagare
Pranete shrinkhal diyechhi pranete
Dekhi ke khulite pare.
...
Jagat majhare yethai bedabi
Yethai basibi yethai dandabi
Ki basante shite, dibase nishithe
Sathe sathe tor thakibe bajite
E pasan pran ananta shrinkhal
Charan jadaye dhare
Ekbar tore dekhechhi yakhan
Kemane edabi more. (ibid.)
[I hear I do not please you:
Let it be.
Like rugged iron ankle-bands
I'll clasp your feet with grappling hands
Eternally.
A wretched captive in my thrall,
I've seized you,
Fettered your life in my life's chains:
Who'll free you?
Wherever you walk in this world,
Wherever sit, wherever stand,
In spring or winter, day or night,
You'll bear the ceaseless clanking weight
Of this hard heart in shackles round your feet....]

Unmistakably the hazy and misty sensation of *Prabhatsangit* is becoming clearer and assuming a distinct and intimate form in the poet's imagination, as if another life, the life eternal, is seeking to mingle with and blossom in his life ephemeral. This fragile and fleeting life is surrounded by eternal life in every season and every direction and in every mood at every moment. The eternal universal life finds expression in the entire cosmic life.

Anantakaler sangi ami tor
Ami ye tor chhaya
Kiba se rodane, kiba se hasite
Dekhite paibe kakhan pashete
Kakhan samukhe kakhan pashchate
Amar adhar kaya
... ...
Ye dike chahibi, akashe amar
Andhar murati anka
Sakali padibe amar adale
*Jagat padibe Dhaka. (*ibid.*)*
[I am your partner for all time, your shadow.
Now in tears and now laughter,
Now before you and now after,
Now beside, my dark shape you will see.
No matter where: look at the skies,
My darkening form will hide the world from sight.]

Another piece from *Chhabi O Gan*, "Nishith Jagat" [World at Night], evokes this *anubhuti* elegantly and eloquently in its poignant presentation of an acutely charged sensation. Clouds are gathering in the western sky, lightning flashing in the cloudy horizon, "bats flying and owls hooting"; in this stormy night a child walks to the forest holding his mother's hand.

Suddenly he frees himself from his mother's clutch in a playful mood and falls behind. The mother calls for her boy and cannot find him. He sits in the forest alone:

Sahasa samukh diyeke galo chhayar mato,
Lagila taras.
Ke jane sahasa yena kotha kondik hate
Shuni dirghashvas.
Ke base rayechhe pashe? Ke chhuinla deha mor
Himhaste tanr? (ibid.)
[Who goes like a shadow all of a sudden
It's eerie.
I know not where I hear a sudden sigh from.
Who's sitting near me? Who's touching me with
A chilly hand?]

Who is this invisible man? He pervades the whole cosmos with all the invisible creatures of the dark. The child has also drowned in the dark vast life universal. He cannot even recognize himself because his own self is submerged in him. It is impossible to see this imprisoned self:

Andhakare apanare dekhite na pai yata
Tata bhalobasi,
Tata tare buke kare bahute bandhiya laye
Harasete bhasi.
Yata yena mane hai pachhe re chalite pathe
Trina phute pai,
Yataner dhan pachhe chamaki kandiya othe
Kusumer ghai. (Ibid.)
[The more I can't see myself in the dark
The more I love him,
The more I hold him in my arm
With delight.
I dread his being stung
By a thorn while walking
Or shocked
(even) by the flower falling on him.]

This "precious treasure" [*yataner dhan*] may be his beloved mate whom he wishes to see:

Sakhare kandiya bale—"Bado sadh yai sakha
Dekhi bhalo kare.
Tui shaishaber bandhu, chirajanma kete galo
Dekhinu na tore.
Bujhi tumi dure achha, ekbar kachhe ese
Dekhao tomai!"
Se amni kende bale—"Apanare dekhi nai
Ki dekhabo tore?" (Ibid.)

[He entreats his mate "It's my only desire to look at you up close, my friend.
You have been childhood companion, and
All my life is spent without seeing you.
I know you stay far away, but come to me
And reveal yourself just for once."
He responds in tears "What could I show
You, alas, I haven't even seen my own self."]

Had he been visible, that *anubhuti* would have vanished in the thin air. His mystery consists in his invisibility. That is why there is so much anxious longing to see him and recognize him.

As I have observed, the very first piece of the poet's collection titled *Manasi* bears testimony to the nexus between his concepts of *Jibandebata* and *bishwajiban*....In "Upahar" [Gift] we get a glimpse of how the waves of life are striking against the poet's heart relentlessly and how the different tunes of bliss and blight of life are resonating inside him....He takes all the music of the vast world outside inside himself and shapes the goddess of his imagination [*manasi-pratima*] with his love and *logos*. This *manasi-pratima* keeps company with him sometimes as a male playmate, sometimes as his dearest female lover, sometimes as his interiorized deity [*antarer debata*] or sometimes as the presiding goddess of life [*jibaner adhisthatri debi*]....

Bahire pathay bishwa katagandha gan drishya
Sangihara saundaryer beshe

Birahi se ghure ghure byathabhara kata sure
Kande hridayer dware ese.
Sei mohamantra gane kabir gabhir prane
Jege uthe birahi bhabana,
Chhadi antahpurabase salajja charane ase
Murtimati marmer kamana.
Antare bahire sei byakulita milanei
Kabir ekanta sukhochhwas
Sei anandamuhurtaguli taba kare dinu tuli
Sarbashrestha praner prakash.
[The world sends out so much beauty in sight, smell, and sound that
Moves about as a forlorn lover and weeps
In piteous melody at the portals of my heart.
This mystical music inspires lover's thoughts [birahi bhabana]
In the innermost core of the poet's heart.
The perfect form of his desire arrives in hesitant steps.
The poet's greatest bliss lies in this passionate union of the outer and the inner.
I dedicate to you those blissful moments as the greatest gift of [my] life.]

Even the last piece in *Manasi* ["Amar Sukh" (My Pleasure)] is worth noticing. The poet feels that he has scored one up over his constant companion residing in him. The latter never enjoyed the aesthetic delight [*madhuri*] that he **did**....The poet believes that he himself has been fused with the world and hence he is infinite and eternal. But he has turned on him who has graciously enabled the poet to have such a realization:

Tumi ki karechha mane dekhechha, peyechha tumi
Simarekha mama?
Pheliya diyachha more adi anta shes kare
Pada punthi sama?
Nai sima agepachhe, yata chao tata ache,
Yatai asibe kachhe tata pabe more.

Amareo diye tumi e bipul bishwabhumi
E akash e batas dite paro bhare.
Amateo sthan peta abadhe samasta taba
Jibaner asha.
Ekbar bhebe dekho e paran dhariachhe
Kata bhalobasa.
("Amar Sukh", *Manasi*])
[Do you think you've fathomed my limit
And discarded me like a book read from beginning to end?
I am unlimited.
You'll have more of me the more you come near me.
You could fill the universe
With my self.
Let all the aspirations of your life
Rest in me.
You need to consider
How my own life harboured
So much love.]

We get to see Rabindranath's mysterious creative impulse as the ideal woman of his imagination in the poet's collection titled *Sonar Tari* [Golden Boat]. My reason for citing this piece is that we get a glimpse of the poet's mysterious creative impulse in it. We noted how a half-familiar being representing all the beauty, smell and movements of the world used to give him company. Though he did not yet get to know know this companion fully, the poet used to have regular tryst with her in his room, on the rooftop under the sky in the morning and in the evening. She was his constant childhood companion as a little girl but now she appears in "Manassundari" [the Pretty Woman of his Imagination] as his lover [*preyasi*] of his adult years. The poet asks:

Mane ache kabe kon phullayuthi bane,
Bahubalyakale, dekha hata dui jane
Adh-chenashona? Tumi ei prithibir

Pratibesinir meye, dharar asthir
Ek balaker sathe ki khela khelate
Sakhi, asite hasiya, tarun prabhate
Nabin balikamurti, shubhrabastra pari
Usar kirandhare sadya snan kari
Bikacha kusumsama phullamukhkhani
Nidrabhange dekha dite niye yete tani
Upabane kudate shephali. Bare bare
Shaishab kartabya hate bhulaye amare,
Phele diye punthi-patra, kede nite khadi,
Dekhaye gopan path dite mukta kari
Pathshala-kara hate; kotha grihakone
Niye yete nirjanete rahasya-bhabane;
Janashunya grihachhade akasher tale,
Bhulate amare, svapnasama chamatkar
Arthahin, satya mithya tumi jana tar.
("Manassundari", *Sonar Tari*)

[Recall the time long ago when we two children
Half-familiar with each other used to have a tryst at
The fully blossomed juthi *grove?*
You, a little girl from a neighboring planet [prithibir pratibeshinir meye,]
Used to play with a restive boy of the earth, clad in a white dress and
Bathed in the bright light of the dawn;
You used to appear as a blossoming flower to awake me
And drag me to the garden to collect shephali *flowers.*
So many times you made me oblivious of my child's chores
And discard my books and you took away my chalk and showed me
The secret alley, thus rescuing me from my school prison-house.

You dragged me to some secret niche of the desolate mysterious

Mansion or the lonely rooftop to play with me or to entertain me

With your wonderful stories under the blue sky; this was like

A wondrous dream that's meaningless and purposeless—you only

Know if these were real or not.]

But the poet's childhood is now over. Even his female playmate has crossed over the juvenile playground. His life is now swayed by the first Spring breeze of mature youth; new aspirations and anxieties as well as the world spirit have touched his heart with new magic and new form. The poet now looks at his childhood companion:

—Khelakshetra hate

Kakhan anatarlakshmi esechha antare,

Apanar antahpure gauraber bhare

Basi achha mahisir mata.

Chhile khelar sangini

Ekhan hayechha marmer gehini,

Jibaner adhisthatri debi. (Ibid.)

[You, the goddess of my heart, have

Left the playground and come gloriously into my heart,

Your own dwelling, where

You sit as my queen.

You were my playmate

But now you've become my soulmate,

The presiding goddess of my life.]

The childhood companion now appears to the poet as his lover.... this innermost lover is no longer confined within him, she has revealed herself in the infinite world of nature outside. The sensation remains the same, though it has taken another form. This indwelling lover can no longer be confused with his inner self, she has blossomed in the infinite world of nature outside. Perhaps she had blossomed in his heart in a previous birth. Though death has snapped the tie their love now pervades the whole universe. Hence the poet beholds the majestic beauty of his lover everywhere in the universe:

Ekhan bhasichha tumi
Ananter majhe; swarga hate martabhumi
Karichha bihar; sandhyar kanakbarne
Rangichha anchal! Usar galitaswarne
Gadichha mekhala; purna tatinir jale
Karichha bistar, taltal chhalchhale
Lalita yaubankhani, basanta-batase
Chanchal basanabyatha sugandha nihshase
Karichha prakash; nisupta purnima-rate
Nirjan gagane, ekakini klanta hate
Bichhaichha dugdha shubhra biraha shayan. (Ibid.)
[You're now hovering in eternity between heaven
And earth; dipping the corner of your garment in
The golden hue of evening; making your girdle
With the molten gold of dawn; mixing and spreading
Your luscious liquid youthful [beauty], and exuding
Your restive pangs of desire in the fragrant breath
Of the spring breeze.
You have spread
The milky white lonesome bed with your
Tired hand in the sleepy desolate
Firmament in the full-moon night.]

However, the poet is unable to find solace and satisfaction in the mere touch of the *anubhuti* of his indwelling lover. He longs to see his *manasi* in real life, and he asks her:

Sei tumi
Murtite dibe ki dekha? Ei martabhumi
Parash karibe ranga charana tale?
Antare bahire bishve shunye jale sthale
Sarba thnai hate, sarbamayi apanare

Kariya haran, dharanir ekdhare
Dharibe ki ekkhani madhur murati? (Ibid.)
[Would you, please, assume a tangible form
And touch this earth under your colorful feet?
Would you take yourself off from all quarters of the
Universe you pervade and
Show your magnificent visage in a
Corner of the earth?]

Anyway, this *anubhuti* of the world of nature never materialized in any tangible form to the poet though he felt touched by its myriad manifestations. One day he wakes up suddenly to find his lover, his "*paran*" [life], as it were, embrace him in trepidation. His heart dances in joy under her unrelenting delightful clutches. Until now he has carefully and tenderly nurtured his *manassundari* lest she is hurt or otherwise importuned, he has smothered her with his passionate kisses and filled her with all that is sweet and charming. In her euphoria she is now senseless to touch and unable to bear the weight of flowers even. But the poet is concerned lest he should lose his charming lover in the bottomless pit of the ocean of dream. He must get her back again.

Bhebechhi ajike khelite haibe
Nutan khela,
Ratribela.
Marandolai dhari rashigachhi
Basiba dujane bado kachhakachhi
Jhanjha asia atta hasia
Maribe thela—
Amar pranete kheliba dujane
Jhulankhela
Nishithbela.
De dol dol!
De dol dol!
E mahasagare tuphan tol

Badhure amar peyechhi abar—
Bharechhe kol.
...
Pranete amate mukhamukhi aj
Chine laba donhe chhadi bhai laj,
Bakshe bakshe parashiba donhe
Bhabe bibhol.
De dol dol.
("Jhulan" [Swing], *Sonar Tari*)
[Hence have I thought to play today
A novel game
In the night-time.
Clutching fast the death-swing's ropes,
The two of us shall nestle close,
The storm will come and give a push
With laughter high:
We two shall play the swinging game
At midnight-time,
My soul and I.
Swing, swing!
Swing, swing!
Raise a tempest on this sea!
My lap is full—my bride again
Has come to me!
Face to Face, my soul and I
Today, all shame and fear laid by,
Will know each other, breast to breast,
On rapture's wing:
Swing, swing!]

We now witness the poet's wondrous *jhulanmela* and the tumult in the his heart as well as in the air and in the sky. However, at another moment this same *manassundari* is dragging him somewhere without a destination [*niruddesh*];

the poet does not even know what is his sojourn for except that he is being led by his indwelling goddess to nowhere. On his way he asks his innermost companion:

Ar kata dure niye yabe more
He sundari?
Balo, kon par bhidive tomar
Sonar tari?
Yakhani shudhai ogo bideshini
Tumi hasa shudhu madhurhasini—
Bujhite na pari, ki jani ki ache
Tomar mane.
Nirabe dekhao anguli tuli
Akul sindhu uthichhe akuli,
Dure pashchime dubichhe tapan
Gagankone
Ki ache hothai-chalechhi kiser
Anvesane?

("Niruddesh Yatra" [Voyage without End], *ibid.*)

[How much further will you lead me, fair one?
Tell me what shore your golden boat will moor on.
Stranger-woman, when I ask
You only smile, sweet-smiling one:
I cannot tell what passes in your mind.
You point a finger silently
Towards the heaving shoreless sea,
The sun upon its western edge inclined.
What waits us there? What do we go to find?]

And yet, the poet was acutely aware that in spite of multiplicities this *anubhuti* has a single undivided reality in him and it is the presence of his *manassundari* or his *Jibandebata...*

Jagater majhe kata bichitra tumi he
Tumi bichitrarupini

[You wear multiple masks
In this variegated world]

... ...

But

Antarmajhe shudhu tumi eka akaki
Tumi antarbyapini
[And yet in my innermost being
You remain as the only and lonely one.] *(*Chitra.*)*

We have seen that the single *anubhuti* of the world of nature has pervaded the poet's interiority as his *manassundari* whom he has found in every manifestation of the life universal and who is giving expression to his life guiding it, straying him off his path at every step on to nowhere. He has no word of his own it being provided by his *manassundari* who is also the presiding deity of his life [*Jibandebata*]. What is this unfathomable mystery, how queer—without purpose, without end!

E ki kautuk nityanutan
Ogo kautukmmayi,
Ami yaha kichhu chahi balibare
Balite ditechha kai!
("Antaryami" [The Innermost One", *ibid.*)
[What prank is this yours,
My mischievous one!
Why don't you let me speak
What I want to say?]

Is that all? Are you making a mockery of my lyric and *logia*? You have also made my life an object of your purposeless fun—I want to go one way and you lead athwart that direction, you have made me a puppet of yours—

Ekada pratham prabhatbelai
Se pathe bahir hainu helai
Mane chhila, din kaje o khelai
Kataye phiriba rate.

But

Pade pade tumi bhulaile dik,

Kotha yaba aj nahi pai thik,

Klantahriday bhranta pathik

Esechhi nutan deshe. *(Chitra)*

[When one morn I went out casually

I thought of spending the day in work and play

And return at night]

But

[You made me forget my way at every step,

I can't find my destination.

I now come to a strange land, a tired and wayward traveler.]

But have you been gratified yet after having accepted my life as the offering for your worship, made me your puppet and an object of your fun and pleasure?

Ohe antaratama,

Mitechhe ki taba sakal tiyas

Asi antare mama.

("Jibandebata", *ibid.*)

If you have made me bankrupt after having possessed my lyric, spirit, and splendor, if your night of love tryst with me is over, then you create me anew so that we start a new tryst. You yourself are ever changing, let your unending playfulness find expression in my transience:

Bhenge dao tabe ajikar sabha,

Ano naba rup ano naba shobha,

Nutan kariya laho arbar

Chirapuratan more. (Chitra)

[Let's be done with our tryst today.

Bring new form and beauty

Make a new man out of my

Familiar old self.]

Yet this novelty has no limit, no end. The grapevine of the poet's life has blossomed due to the touch of this indwelling one. He again invokes this *antaratama* in his life:

Tumi esa nikunja nibase
Esa mor sarthank sadhan.
Lute lao bharia anchal
Jibaner sakal sambal,
Nirabe nitanta abanata
Basanter sarba samạrpan.
Hasimukhe niye yao yata
Baner bedan nibedan. (Chaitali)
[Come, enter my grove
O my fulfillment!
Take away my life's spring treasures
Humbly and silently offered.
Take all the pain and pangs of this
Grove with a smile.]

We have endeavored to get to know the *anubhuti* of life in Rabindranath's poetical career from the composition of *Prabhatsangit* to *Chaitali.* Though numerous poems of his provide a glimpse of this *anubhuiti,* those bearing a clearer stamp of it help us comprehend this wondrous mystery. We noted that from the beginning of his literary career the poet demonstrates a close connection between his inner sensibilities and the myriads of manifestations of the external world of nature.

Moreover, he visualizes with his eyes or in his imagination [*maner dristi*], hears, and feels with his touch a bird's song, wind's murmur, the sun, the moon and the stars in the firmament, human movements, trees and shrubs, rivers, and everything else—they all have gathered in his innermost being. He is partially familiar with this holistic form and yet it is his constant companion. However, this undivided form cannot realize itself within the confines of the poet's interiority; it seeks to mingle with the wider world outside. The pieces of *Prabhatsangit* express this aspiration. As I mentioned earlier, the hazy presence of this indwelling being gradually achieves a distinct profile. Appearing initially as a composite of the multiplicities of the world of nature it goes on to become the poet's playmate, his intimate consort—the childhood companion becomes the presiding deity of his heart in his youth and ultimately his beloved spouse [*marmer grihini*]. This marital game [*dampatyalila*] could become tiresome and boring from time to time requiring a fresh start or it could raise occasional doubts about its success or satisfaction. However, this *manassundari* is more than just the poet's lover—she is his *jibaner adhisthatri debi.*

Really speaking, the realization of this supreme governor, the lord of life, on the poet's life is *eo ipso* a wondrous and mysterious aesthetic presence. This is because his *Jibandebata* is a wonderful representation as well as the realization of the cosmic life. As he is connected to the cosmos by an umbilical cord, as it were, he easily and elegantly finds an aesthetic pleasure in the most trivial natural objects and phenomena. The poems and lyrics of the poet's *opus* beginning with the *Prabhatsangit*through *Katha O Kahini* [Story and History], *Kalpana* [Imagination], *Kshanika* [Momentary] contain no somber philosophy or rhetoric but and unlimited reserve of unalloyed beauty and music.

The poems of this phase of the poet's life illuminate the joy emanating from a complete union between the outer and the inner, between earthly life and cosmic life. The [poet's] entire life is drowned in the beauty, love, and enjoyment of the world of nature—as if he is spiritedly seeking to lose himself in the ever flowing beauty of cosmic life. We sense the *Sturm und Drang* of this gushing sentiment in such pieces as "Basundhara' [Earth], "Yete Nahi Diba" [I Won't Let You Go], "Samudrer Prati" [To the Ocean], "Swarga Haite Bidai" [Farewell to Paradise], and "Prabasi" [Emigrant]. His *anubhuti* is arguably wonderfully uncanny.

Trine pulakita ye matir dhara
Lutai amar samne
Se amake dake eman kariya

Kena ye kaba ta kemane?
Mane hai yena se dhulir tale
Yuge yuge ami chhinu trina jale
Se duar khuli kabe kon chhale
Bahir hayechhi bhramane.
...
E satmahala bhabane amar
Chirajanamer bhitate
Sthale jale ami hajar bandhane
Bandha ye githate githate.
(Sonar Tari)

[I can't express how
The grass-laden earth beacons to me!
I feel as if I have wandered out
Of the door [of my home]
Behind which I had lived for ages
Under the dust, in the grass, and in the water.
...
In this grand mansion,
My eternal home,
I remain tied
Knot by knot on land and in water.]

It is common knowledge that Rabindranath's poetical career starting from *Prabhatsangit* down to *Kalpana* and *Kshanika* is primarily an aesthetic experience. Thereafter begins a new chapter in his life starting with *Naibedya* [Offerings] and *Kheya* [Ferry], when the poet parts company with his blissful aesthetic interaction with nature. There is pain in this parting and it finds expression in several poems of *Kalpana* and *Kshanika*. However, the *anubhuti* of *Jibandebata* still lingers in the poet's heart. Yet, alas, it's time say good bye to his *manassundari*:

Ami nisthur kathin kathor
Nirmam ami aj
Ar nahi deri bhairab bheri

Bahire uthichhe baji.
Tumi ghumaichha nimil nayane
Kanpiya uthichha biraha shayane
Prabhate uthiya shunya nayane
Kandiya chahia rabe...
[I am relentless and unsparing today.
The terrible drum is beating outside,
There's no time.
You're sleeping with eyes shut
But you shiver in the pang of separation.
You'll wake up weeping at dawn
With a vacant look ...]

The poet is well aware, and yet—

Samai hayechhe nikat ekhan
Bandhan chhindite habe.
(Kalpana)
[It's time now To cut the knot of the tie.]

The poet's parting with his aesthetic life is complete in *Naibedya.* His close connection with the world of nature could no longer be felt. There will be no realization of beauty in the most trivial and tiny objects; there will be no occasion "to see a world in a grain of sand," no moments to savor the sheer bliss of experiencing the sublime; this world of joys and jitters, smiles and sorrows will no longer move the poet's heart. This new phase of his poetic career reaches its acme in *Gitanjali* [Song Offerings] and *Gitimalya* [Garland of Songs]. It is the lord of world spirit who now presides over the poet's new life. We notice a sea change in the poet's thoughts about his *Jibandebata.* His heart and soul now remain absorbed in deeper mysteries than his communion with world life. The poet's *anubhuti* of *jibandebata*, that is contingent upon his intimacy with world life, is yielding place to a higher arcana.

We will understand this change better if we bear in mind that consciousness of the world life or spirit is not quite the same as consciousness of the lord of the world. Admittedly, the consciousness of world life and the consciousness of the lord of the world are related. Yet we must not confuse the two. *Jibandebata* expresses himself not in world life but in individual life. He enacts his *lila* in the interiority of the individual human being who realizes him in the external world. We realize our temporal life in the world life by the grace of *Jibandebata*. This is because our life is connected to the world life—"we share the same rhythm" and that is why we feel in our life the pulsation of the life universal. In this sense, *Jibandebata* is actually a deeper and larger extension of the poet's own life. However, this is not exactly Rabindranath's understanding of god or the lord of the world. Yet it seems that for him the *Jibandebata* consciousness merged gradually with that of world spirit and he was led to the realization of the lord of the world or god through his identification with the cosmic life. There are sparks of thoughts of the divine in some of the poems of *Kheya, Gitanjali, and Gitimalya.*

My analysis of the mysteries of Rabindranath's poetic life highlights a simple truth of which I have tried to provide but a faint hint. Perhaps the *mysterium tremndum* of his *Jibandebata* underlies this truth. I do not think it necessary to unravel the mysteries of Rabindranath's poetic consciousness through such lofty philosophies as monism or Hegelianism. The poet's mystery belongs primarily to the affective domain....Rabindranath is a poet *par excellence* and not a pedantic scholar. The font of his poetic consciousness is neither an identifiable philosophy nor esoteric knowledge about truth, but rather his extraordinary spontaneous capacity for feeling. This faculty has enabled him to unravel the inscrutable mysteries of life—*na medhaya na vahudha shrutena* [neither by ratiocination nor with the help of profound philosophies]. Hence I do not try to search for a theory or a philosophy to explain the mystery of *Jibandebata* as I do not think any such theorizing will help us know the poet or grasp his output.

But let me return to the theme of our discourse. Is it really the case that the poet of *Kalpana* or *Kshanika* lost the wonderful *anubhuti* of his *manassundari* or *Jibandebata*? Apparently, the poet seems to have lost it. Would the poet's beloved *manassundari* who lived inside the poet's heart be lost forever? Would the lord of the world replace his lord of life [*bishwadebata*]?

It is fairly known that Rabindranth, the composer of *Gianjali-Gitimalya-Gitali*, found a new life in *Balaka* [The Crane]. This "born again" experience of the poet is truly wonderful. We used to think that Rabindranath finally eschewed his aesthetic sensibilities of *Gitanjali-Gitimalya* and surrendered himself to the feet of *Bishvadebata*. Indeed this would been the normal evolution of human nature. But this was not the case with Rabindranath. I have discussed this elsewhere and do not wish to repeat my arguments here. *Balaka* is poetry of restlessness and movement celebrating love, youth, and beauty with a high intellectual appeal. The poet's *Jibandebata* tantalizingly larks behind this motion and emotion of love, youth, and beauty. "*Matta sagar padi dila gahan ratrikale, ai ye amar neye*" ["My helmsman set sail in turbulent sea at the dead of night"]—we hear the faint footsteps of this stranger, the man in the heart [of the poet] in this line. *Balaka* is followed by *Palataka* [The Fugitive] which testifies to the poet's concern with the mundane multiple trials and tribulations, and the weal and woes of human life, which is a part of universal life. It seems that his poems in *Palataka* seek to probe the varied experiences of life through the variegated emotions and sentiments of human heart expressed in them. It is becoming clear that the consciousness of his female playmate of childhood, companion of his adolescence, and the pretty princess of his youthful imagination mysterious and inscrutable, approaches slowly closer to his heart's sanctum. Ever she comes, she comes.

In fact she arrives in *Purabi* [titled after an Indian musical note], in spite of the poet's deeper consciousness of the lord of the universe. This is because world life is dearer than the lord of the world to Tagore. Rabindranath is a poet of human and universal life. I have discussed the deeper thoughts of *Purabi* elsewhere, though I find it necessary to reproduce some parts of my critique here. For whatever reasons, Rabindranath's poetic career that had been grounded in deep spiritual thoughts staged a comeback to his deep engagement with the smiles and sorrows, with the water, dust, grass, and tress of this sacred earth: "*punya dharar dhulomati phal hawa jal trina tarur sane.*"

Ei ya dekha ei ya chhonwa, ei bhalo ei bhalo
Ei bhalo aj e sangame kannahasir ganga yamunai
Dheu kheyechhi dub thiechhi ghat bharechhi niyechhi bedai.
Ei bhalore praner range ei asanga sakal ange mane.
Punya dharar dhulomati phal hawa jal trina tarur sane. (Purabi)
[That I have seen, touched, dived in the
Confluence of joys and sorrows, and filled my pitcher
And have bid farewell—this is enough.
I am blessed that I have shared
My body and soul with the water, dust, grass, and trees of this sacred earth.]

Now the poet could easily feel:

Aj dharani apan hate
Anna dilen amar pate
Phal diyechhen sajiye patrapute
Ajke mather ghase ghase
Nihshwase mor khabar ase
Kothai achha bishwajaner pran. (ibid.)
[(Mother) earth served me
Food with [her] own hand today.
(She) has put the fruits on plates of leaves
The meadows bring my news in every grass
Where are you the vital force of the universe?]

This echoes the thoughts of his youth—a desire to feel the universal life within his own. The resurgence of this feeling also ensures the return of the poet's playful companion, his *manassundari*. She has come:

Duar bahire yemani chahire
Mane hala yena chini

Kabe, nirupama ogo priyatama
Chhile lilasangini. (ibid.)
[I look outside of my door
And feel as if I recognize you.
When did you, my dearest one,
*Play with me last?] (*Purabi *)*

This playmate had met the poet many, many times in the past, opening his doors, and charming him in various guises—sometime as newly bloomed flower or sometimes as newly formed cloud. She has come back at the fag end of the poet's life. Would he be able to welcome her to his home?

Dekho na ki hai, bela chale yai
Sara haye ela din
Baje purabir chhande rabir
Shes raginir bin.
Etadin hetha chhinu ami parabasi,
Hariye phelechhi sediner banshi
Aj sandhyay pran othe nihshwasi
Ganhara udasin.
Kena abelay dekechhe khelay
Sara haye ela din. (ibid.)
[Alas, time is rolling by
The day is coming to its end;
The sun's lute is playing
The final note in the Purabi melody.
I have been a stranger here so long
I have lost the flute I had.
My heart is heavy with melancholy without any music.
Why has she summoned me to play [with her]
When the day is coming to an end?
At the end of the day?] (Purabi)

In several pieces of *Purabi* we notice the poet's unmistakable expression of his recovery of the consciousness of his lover of imagination (*manasipriya*), his lord of life (*Jibandebata*). The aesthetic delights that had filled his earlier life with bliss and then had been lost have crept stealthily and silently into the realm of his imagination and thoughts in the poet's later life....

Aj dekhi sediner sei kshin padadhvani tar
Amar ganer chhanda gopane karichhe adhikar,
Dekhi tar adrishya anguli
Svapna ashru sarobare kshane kshane dei dheu tuli.
(ibid.)

[I now know the sound of her faint footsteps of yore
Have mysteriously possessed my lyrics,
I also see her unseen fingers causing ripples in the
Tear-filled lake of my dream.] (Purabi)

The poet's lover gave her parting kiss long ago. He has almost forgotten it in the hiatus of the long separation. But he now remembers her and asks her forgiveness piteously for his lapse of memory. How many leaves of *madhabi* flower wilted, how many noons noisy with dove song, how many evenings have left their golden amnesia, how many nights have written an obscure script and lapsed in oblivion after that last kiss. Even if the poet asks forgiveness of his long lost beloved, he nevertheless is fully aware that his lover, his *Jibandebata,* has already blessed his life with her touch.

Tabu jani. Ekdin tumi dekha diyechhile bale
Ganer phasale mor e jiban uthechhila phale.
Ajo nai shes
... ...
Tomar parash nahi ar
Kintu ki parashmani rekhe gechha antare amar
Bishver amrita chhabi ajio to dekha dey more
Kshane kshane akaran anander sudhapatra bhare
Amare karay pan. (ibid.)

[I know my life blossomed in songs because
You came to me.
It's still not empty yet
... ...

Though I miss your touch
I know I carry your touchstone inside me
I still behold the immortal visage of the world
And drink the cup of gratuitous bliss every moment.]
(Purabi)

...I have tried to unravel the mystery and mystique of Rabindranath's *jibandebata* according to my own understanding. My explanation may not be valid even. Yet, I must conclude by claiming that the font of Tagore's sensibilities enriching his poetic career and filling it with variegated forms and fragrance is, undeniably, his consciousness of universal life. This consciousness colored his childhood, adolescence, and youth, and the same consciousness brings a twilight tinge to fill the sunset hours of his life.

Without daring to take my eyes off him, I climbed onto the verandah and said, "Sit down. I'll get you something to eat." We gave him a few mangoes. I sat down on the deck-chair and wondered what to do next. The man looked harmless, but how would I go to sleep with a madman outside my door? The servants did not sleep in the house, there was nobody around to carry a message. It did not seem that the man intended to depart soon. Having finished the mangoes, he settled down comfortably. I would have been happy to keep him busy with some more food, but there was nothing more in the house. What were we to do now? We decided to wait for the guards to arrive on their nightly rounds around Santiniketan. They should have come, but tonight when we needed them, they were late. The minutes passed; we could see neither their flashlights nor hear their whistles. I sat there. Not far away, Miss Petit slept on peacefully. Jyotirmoybabu tried to rouse her, but she only said, "Oh, he is mad, he won 't hurt us". Then she turned over and went back to sleep.

But our dark night's visitor showed no signs of leaving. Nor did it seem a good idea to let him go without ascertaining his destination. If pleased with our services, how long would it be before his return? Faced with no other option, we decided to enlist Miss Petit's help. This time, Makshirani woke her up and explained the situation. She immediately appeared, dressed in a black kimono. She jumped off the veranda and briskly went up to the intruder,

'You want to meet Rabindranath Thakur? Come with me, I will take you to him.' At first, the man stood silent and motionless. Saying

'Come, come, come with me', the fearless woman almost dragged him away and disappeared with him into the dark fields. We two intrepid knights of Bengal, stood aside and watched. Ultimately Jyotirmoybabu accompanied Miss Petit, though it served no purpose other than saving face, and I stayed to guard the family. They soon returned, having turned him over to the watchman at Uttarayan. We slept restfully that night, heartened by the presence of a very brave woman next door.

From then on, it was arranged that a gardener would sleep in the house; we also realised that the guards had been instructed to keep a close watch over us. But we did not have to suffer such a night-time intrusion again. Insanity though seemed to be in the air, for another mad person graced Uttarayan with her presence the next day, a woman this time. She came from Burdwan by train, carrying a cat in her arms, covered with her sari like a baby. She sent message, "Go tell Bouthan that Sarala Debi has come fro m Jorasanko." She took Pratima Debi by surprise. Though mad, she was still in possession of some sense, and seemed well-informed; her eyes rested with keenness on many of the articles lying around the house. She did not seem prepared to go away with empty hands, so she was given some money, taken to the Bolpur station and put on the train.

One day we heard that a cobra had its den below a neem tree near the Ratan Kuthi kitchen—the servants saw it all the time; once Kashi had only just missed stepping on it. Almost on cue, we began to be showered with innumerable stories about local snakes. Once, a certain gentleman was staying in the same room that we were in now. He was working at the table one day when something fell from above with a thud.

Startled, he looked up to see a snake. When he looked up at the ceiling, he saw another one peeping out. prema-murati hridaye jage, ananda nahi dhare.

(Sinking in a sea of nectar, I forget the world, sun and moon disappear.

I see no country, no history, no border -an image of love awakes in my heart, I cannot contain my joy.)

It captures the spirit of the original and at the same time works on its own as a beautiful poem. One could not ask for more

A Foreign Shine and Assumed Gestures: The Ersatz Tagore of the West between the arms of the Beloved, in the ecstasy of love's joy:

Bring the tearful streams of the rainy clouds to your eyes, and cover your heart with the shadow of darkness:

Bring your face nearer to His ear, and speak of the deepest longings of your heart.

Kabir says: "Listen to me, brother! bring the vision of the Beloved in your heart."

Crisis in Civilization, and a Poet's Alternatives: Education as one alternative weapon

Under the present circumstances it may not sound like an old fashioned romantic cliché if someone declares today, that the aim of all education is to seek a world where mankind can co-exist with nature in an atmosphere of fearless warmth, trust and freedom.

A poet may naturally claim that finding joy in the simple things of life, and compassion for our fellow creatures are the basic values upon which small children's education should be founded, as these happen to hold the secret of creative energy. It dose not sound far fetched because joy and compassion are also the ultimate end of civilization.

What we are doing to ourselves today throughout the world, is driving this planet towards the final moment, where all creation ends, and destruction takes over. Creativity is god's gift to mankind, it cannot grow freely when it is used as a tool for hatred, as creativity is by definition contrary to destruction. Awareness of the responsibilities of being human and of our human failures is the foundation upon which creativity rests.

I am trying to examine how far a poet can foresee a crisis that a civilization might *face, of which education is an important component,* and how, as a sensitive, creative, responsible human being he can think of possible alternatives to counteract the dangers. A poet has positive dreams for this universe. He is also practical and pragmatic, because he cares for this universe. With his knowledge rooted in reality and his instinct and imagination flying into the distant future, he has a shrewd understanding of the course that human history is about to take and is pained and worried about the future of mankind that his poet's vision can foresee.

Our poet used his visionary imagination to predict and to solve the dangers that western civilization was creating for itself and for the rest of the world, *because the east was emulating its ways partly by choice, and partly by choice, and partly through values imposed by colonial educational policies.*

The so-called mystic saint could very clearly see the logical, practical conclusions of a dangerous process that had already begun its course. And he tried to offer practical solutions, tried to change the course of history as far as he could by spreading his anxious thoughts far and wide and by actively working with the people. *Rabindranath was very much of an educational activist as we understand the term today.* He saw education as a holistic device which prepared a complete human being for the betterment of the world. It was expected to build a child's values right from the beginning.

An incorrigible pacifist, the poet protested against all war and violence, denounced terrorism even when the young men were risking their lives fighting to free his own country. In those emotionally charged days of nationalist movement he wrote very strongly against the very concept of nationalism, as a divisive element created by western technology that disturbed peaceful coexistence, and encouraged hostility among countries by fanning self-pride. So he talked about connectivity, and internationalism. He wanted his students to imbibe all these values, and possess an inner eye, in order to build a better world based not on separatism and self-pride but on togetherness and mutual trust.

Rabindranath was one of the earliest environmentalists in today's world, who began the act of afforestation to protect the land from erosion, wrote powerful songs about it to spread the message, and had made planting of trees into an annual festival in his school more than seventy five years ago.

A secular educationist per se, he created secular festivities in his school which could be shared by students of all religions. Realising the social and educational significance of sharing rituals and of enjoying festivals together, he invented secular festivals for the old and the young.

There were festivities in his school to celebrate the coming of every season. *Barsho Shesh* and *Naba barsho* for summer, *Barshaa Mangal* for monsoon, *Sharadotsab* for Autumn, *Basantotsab* for Spring. And he encouraged *Paush Mela,* the winter fair introduced by his father Maharshi Debendranath which celebrated the harvest time and brought the rural and the urban together, by making the interchange of culture and commerce possible between the two.

All these were integral parts of Tagore's educational policy, which stretched well beyond the limits of his school, to ways of building future citizens of the world.

Just as introducing the cooperative system in the rural areas was his way of educating the rural poor to function together, in order to earn a livelihood. Taking his lessons from the European farmers, he began a cooperative movement for the *adivasis* in the rural areas, the *samabaayika,* a cooperative banking system for the rural areas.

Disgusted by the flawed colonial education system that was imposed upon Indian children, he offered an alternative schooling system. *The western mode of education, he felt, was more harmful than helpful for us, it steamrolled the children into artificial discipline, taught textbooks that were meant for children of an unfamiliar culture, an unfamiliar climate, forced them to learn too many things by rote without touching base.* It did not reflect the reality of the students' lives. The foreign dress code, for example, was unsuitable for a warm climate, it also kept them away from being in touch with nature and their natural surroundings. So, in his experimental school the students wore comfortable Indian clothes, walked barefoot, to feel the ground beneath their feet, and classes were held in the open air under the shade of trees. The students were encouraged to be creative, to sing, draw, paint, sculpt, dance, act, tell stories, write poetry, cherish open spaces, as well as enjoy a huge playground and a well furnished library. So much for their body and their mind. The prayer meetings in the morning took care of their spirits.

Education could not be complete without knowing your own cultural roots.

Though not a trained anthropologist, but a sensitive and farsighted man, Rabindranath was instinctively aware of the value of preserving tribal culture. Therefore while trying to solve the dire economic needs of the *adivasis,* and educating them in health, agriculture, savings and other modern day practical ways of survival, he encouraged undisturbed preservation of their own tribal culture without interfering with their basic lifestyle.

Tagore wanted a system of education that would bring his people the best of both worlds, the East and the West, the rural and the urban, the ancient and the contemporary. Yes, a poet can cherish such a dream, and take on its responsibilities, and more.

Tagore was rubbishing the concept of the Nation as a selfish product of western technology that harmed peace by promoting difference. Instead of spreading cooperation, communication and consideration, it promoted suspicion, competition and coercion, and instigated violent passions and hostilities. Like nation, the concepts of race, religion and ethnicity, also divide mankind into warring groups and we urgently need a loose, broad state structure, the concept of

"No–Nation," to accommodate all in their own space. Any civilization that rests upon dividing up people, carries the seed of its own destruction within itself. Proper education within the right value system would open the inner eye and make people see the truth.

And political power, he wrote, was dependent on economic power and could not be separated from it. Tagore warned us of a world where "the greed to possess more and more things" (the term 'consumerism' was not yet known) and a demand and supply policy that creates artificial demand among people to possess more and more material goods will bring about a day when technology will destroy the earth. He could foresee a time when *western civilization would lead itself and the rest of the world to destruction.*

If our education had its roots in Indian culture, he genuinely believed, it could teach mankind how to rise above these misleading divisive notions, and peacefully co-exist.

Rabindranath felt that in India the colonial education system was imposed form above, the strong discipline in the schools was based on fear, not on sympathy. The mechanically imposed system did not take account of the individual students' state of mind or body, it forced its rules upon them, ultimately killing their souls.

Tota kahini "The Parrot's Tale" is a shattering piece on the abuse of student by an inhuman education system. It is a powerful satire expressing his disapproval of the heartless notion of forced formal education as it was applied in India. An alienated system that took a cruel pride in self and did not care for the other's reality.

Instead of liberating and enriching the mind, mindless colonial education chained it, separated it form its natural surroundings, stole its joy of life and killed its soul, thus ultimately defeating the sole purpose of education.

In fact he saw western civilization itself as a civilization based on war and fear and *not* on empathy. Education system was an integral part of it. He predicted in the voice of a seer, about war, long before fascism and ethnic murder appeared in

Europe—"Those who are constantly developing their instinct of fight and the intolerance of aliens will be eliminated." he wrote (*Nationalism p. 97*). A situation had been created when "a watchful attitude of animosity against Others was taken as a solution to their problems."

Tagore knew in his heart, that this was no permanent solution to human problems. "We are confronted with two alternatives," he wrote, "it will be interminable competition, or cooperation." (*p. 101*). And competition was what Western education system pampered, not cooperation.

Worried about the connected sources of power in the western civilization, industry, commerce, and military, Tagore called the system "the gigantic organization for hurting others and for warding off their blows" (and poor man had no idea then in 1916 how many billions of dollars would be spent in the world for the purpose of Defense, in another 50 years time.)

"Only those people have survived and achieved civilization", he wrote, "who have the spirit of cooperation strong in them." (*p. 99-100*)

The goal of all education, he felt, was to create this spirit of cooperation in human mind. To connect people, to protect and promote human civilization.

The western notion of education, he was afraid, installed wrong values in children. It fanned their sense of separateness, whereas India, he firmly believed, had a better alternative to offer its students, "the spirit of co-operation." which was at the root of human civilization.

Forever our contemporary, Rabindranath had worried about Globalization as well. Addressed by his countrymen as *Bishwa Kabi,* a World Poet, he had always perceived human consciousness as one. A sense of the wholeness of the world rules his heart as well as his mind.

Tagore had commented (as early as in 1916) that although the western civilization stressed separateness, rather than unity, nevertheless, science and technology were bringing the world together. "The whole world is becoming one country through scientific facility. And the moment is arriving when you also must find a basis of unity which is not political." (*p. 99*).

This basis he felt, had to be *a moral power* which alone could hold the center together for mankind. *By moral power he meant "the higher instincts of sympathy and mutual help." (p. 99) Education was meant to develop this moral power of sympathy in mankind.*

But was western education system achieving this end? The first world war had started, when Tagore wrote, "The people who are lacking in this higher moral power, and who therefore cannot combine in fellowship with one another, must perish or live in a state of degradation" (*p.99*)

Nearly a century later, needless to say, we are living upon this planet in a state of perpetual, pitiful degradation, because the world has not succeeded in "combining in fellowship" as the poet wanted.

The keyword to solve the crisis in human civilization, for Rabindranath, perhaps, was transparency. Openness was all. No secret spying outfits, no shutting out of aliens through strict immigration laws, no secret societies for political activists, even if it is for human rights and the independence of a country. Open up your heart, and have an open mind, you'll solve most of your problems. Open up all your doors and windows, in your mind, in your politics, in your trade, in your culture. Let ideas freely flow through the peoples of the world, let us all be in touch, and exchange thoughts. *This was the ultimate aim of education.*

Education should allow us to welcome fresh air into our closed spaces, and break down artificial barriers, because, he felt, real differences among mankind should be recognized not glossed over, nor bulldozed into oneness, yet an overall unity does exist and should be respected.

It needs emotional and intellectual sympathy and cooperation. And this, the poet believed was the whole object of human civilization. Without intellectual sympathy one race can never understand the problems of another. *The British system of education in India, lacked emotional as well as intellectual sympathy. Tota Kahini is a picture of that terrible lacunae that leads to the failure of the system.*

In this context Rabindranath juxtaposed two basic concepts that guide us today, competition and cooperation. One leads to war and the other leads to peace. *The western education system was one that encouraged competition. Tagore wanted to create a fresh education system which will emphasize cooperation.*

The course that human history has taken in the 20th century would have pained Rabindranath no doubt but would not have taken him by surprise. Although he had not heard the words that we live with, like the holocaust, or Hiroshima, the My Lai, or Bosnia, the Green House Effect, or 9/11, and he did not live to see his country divided into three nations, knew neither Khomeini nor Laden, neither Bush nor Modi, — yet he knew exactly which route history was taking, and had tried to warn the world. And to protect this from self-destruction.

Tagore knew the deadly effects of suspicion, fear and hatred among nations, as well as communities, of fundamentalism, and ethnic pride. The heating of the planet through thoughtless deforestation, and poisoning of the earth, water and sky through technology, all this he had known through his visionary's eyes. Imagining the uncertain future of a shortsighted, self-defeating mankind, he had nightmares which were expressed in his last speech, *Crisis in Civilization.*

And all his life Rabindranath had searched for and found a million ways to offer us positive alternatives to counter them. *Creating a new system of education was only one of them.*

In Bangla storytelling formula, a tale begins, *Ek je chhilo raja,* ("There was a king"). In one of his last pieces written in 1941, just before his death, he begins his tale with this formulaic expression *Ek je achhe manush* ("There is a man"). He makes two enormously important changes in the formula, he changes its tense from the past to the present, and changes its subject from a king to a common man.

Instead of *"there was"* he writes *"there is",* and instead of *"a king"* he writes *"a man",* meaning a *human being.*

These were the alternatives he offered to mankind, to grapple with the crisis our civilization had created for itself, and the world was passing through in 1941. The focus was to be shifted from the past *to the present,* not the *present moment* but the continuous presence, *bartaman,* indicating the eternal presence of mankind upon this planet. And also a shift from the royalty to the common man, from the source of political power, to the source of moral strength.

Not freedom from history, nor submission to it, but continuous adjustment to its needs, trying to *mould* its course, is what we need for the survival of the human spirit.

And that, Tagore believed, was what real education ought to prepare us for.

Let him speak in his own voice.

At a time when interest in Rabindranath Tagore, also in the non-English speaking West, may be said to be entering a new phase, with the promise of a wider readership both inside and outside academic circles, all three of Uma Das Gupta's books, published in impressive succession of each other, carry a weighty significance. From the point of view of contemporary global history too, which numerous scholars across the board of humanities have rightly perceived as having entered a new cycle of imperialism, Tagore's idea(l)s offer much scope for important reappraisal. The three books by Uma Das Gupta on Tagore, two of which are biographies and the third an edited collection of letters, are an important contribution in this direction.

Biography is an art in itself. Not unlike literary translation, it requires its author to be able to read as a critic and write as a writer. Uma Das Gupta succeeds on both counts. Her works dealing with the life of the Bengali polymath are an outcome of years of careful research and extensive reading. While in her short biography of Tagore, her voice is clearly in the forefront, in *Rabindranath Tagore: my life in my words*, she is, as it were, a hidden presence. Her style is engaging, achieving a fine balance which satisfies the general reader and specialist alike. Moreover, her longstanding involvement with

Santiniketan, going back to her parents' close association with Tagore, gives her writing an intimacy that brings the reader even closer to the subject.

For a Tagore biography to succeed, however, there is yet another requirement. It is suggested by Tagore's own scepticism towards retelling life's events as they supposedly *really* happened. Even in the case of autobiography, they are of necessity artistic recreations, in Tagore's case captivatingly so. A sensitive biographer is therefore urged to adopt an approach that is concerned less with the chronicling of external events than with elaborating ideas which informed the artist's long and creative life. Uma Das Gupta clearly takes this as her guideline in organising the contents of both the biographies, a point she makes in her Introduction to *Rabindranath Tagore: my life in my words*: "In the final analysis, [Tagore's] life history is mainly a biography of ideas and artistic creations." Ideas, in Tagore's world, take precedence over life's happenings, though his life was astoundingly rich in both.

The main ideas explored in *Rabindranath Tagore; A Biography* are those of the poet as an educator and rural reformer and not so much as a writer and poet. This choice seems in part pragmatic, dictated by the author's own area of expertise (her knowledge of the history of Tagore's institution of Visva-Bharati in Santiniketan). At the same time it is motivated by presenting the lesser covered sides of Tagore and his many concerns. Finally, there were the constraints imposed by the OUP biographies series, with its objective that the life histories of men and women who contributed towards building modern India be short.

Thus in just over a hundred pages of ten concisely written chapters, packed with information (sometimes gleaned also from oral sources), the life of Tagore is portrayed through a series of interrelated themes, such as nationalism, internationalism, lessons from India's history, the need for an alternative, world-encompassing education, a search for self-esteem, to mention the main ones. What we are presented with, is, in Uma Das Gupta's formulation, "an indefatigable man of action": a founder of a school and a university, a pioneer in rural reconstruction work, an untiring globe-trotter out on a mission, in other words a man struggling every step of the way to make a difference in the lives of his countrymen and "bring change", in what small way he could, "to an unequal and unjust world". Oftentimes against great odds and little understanding both at home and abroad, Tagore is seen to emerge as what another eminent scholar William Radice has termed a "one-man counter-culture".

If Uma Das Gupta's biography extends the portrayal of Tagore beyond the common perception of him as a poet and writer – and the subject of Tagore's creative writing is dealt within fewer than ten pages – there is certain poetic justice in that she closes the biography with a poem. The social consciousness in Tagore was never separate from his artistic consciousness; the man of action was never far from the contemplative man. The ethical source from which both drew was essentially the same: "a universal humanist outlook". This was the imaginative ideal, the biography makes clear, in terms of which Rabindranath was ceaselessly moving, with many twists and turns on the way, from occasionally quite traditionalist beginnings, but over the years through ever-widening sympathies and sensibilities as both a man and poet.

Closing the biography with a poem which bespeaks a strong a sense of remoteness, even failure, in the face of the world's vast impenetrable demands, serves also another point. It shows Tagore at his most vulnerable and human. The poem's selection seems almost strategic in that it resists the temptation for a larger-than-life portrayal of the poet, as it also importantly suggests a point of contact between him and our own individual lives. "I believe that if we can inwardly relate to this poem", says Uma Das Gupta, "we shall find he is there as a friend in our lives helping us to live with honesty in our weaknesses and our strengths." That is surely the best way to keep Tagore's legacy meaningful and alive.

One of the many strengths of this short biography is the wide assortment of citations, sourced from Tagore's own writings but also from those of others, with which Uma Das Gupta weaves the threads of the main body of her text into a tight and multicoloured fabric. Each and every chapter is preceded by at least two pithy quotations, which help set the tone and drive her point home. It seems she misses no opportunity to give Tagore – or anyone else deserving, for that matter – a chance to speak. Even her decision to confine herself to selecting letters for the *Appendix* from the body of his letters written in English is guided by her desire "to represent him in his own words". Language too is no barrier: where English translation is unavailable or inadequate, she resorts to her own translation skills and opens another chink for the non-Bengali readers to appreciate Tagore more fully.

All these skills come to bear more fully in her *Rabindranath Tagore: my life in my words*, a book of almost four hundred pages. Although this project was initiated by Penguin books and not the author herself (she was invited to "write" Tagore's autobiography), it feels as though it had grown organically from her shorter biography. The sources she draws on and translates from are vast and impressive. She had not only plumbed the Rabindra Bhavana archives in Santiniketan but also the Department of Western Manuscripts of the Bodleian Library (University of Oxford) and Senate House Library (London) for the papers of Tagore's various English correspondents. To know that only the Santiniketan archives house close to six thousand letters is to get a sense of the Herculean task she undertook.

There are as many as 117 entries translated by her from the original Bengali, nearly all of which appear here for the first time in English. Only a few of the letters to his wife and children had previously appeared in Krishna Dutta's and Andrew Robinson's translation in their *Selected Letters of Rabindranath Tagore*. Those who do not read Bengali, but love Tagore and want to access as much of his writing as possible will be extremely pleased by this turnout. In the meantime, another important autobiographical work, *Âtmaparichay*, which Uma Das Gupta draws on and translates from, has also appeared for the first time in a full English translation.

Having more than one translation at hand to draw on is always useful. It gives a fuller, and more contested, picture of what for non-Bengali speakers must remain an unattainable original. The site of contestation opened up by the two different translations of some of Tagore's letters to his family, particularly to his wife, is indeed interesting. It raises questions that seem to divide opinion among Bengalis to this day. Consider this example from one of the letters Tagore wrote to Mrinalini Devi. In Uma Das Gupta's translation, the passage reads:

Please don't work any harder for my happiness. Your love is enough. But it would be very nice if you and I could work together and think together with one mind. I know that cannot always happen even if we wish it [...] I don't wish to leave you *out* of anything. Everyone has the right to do things their own way, as they would like to. *It may not be possible for you to agree with my wishes and inclinations every time* – I would not worry about it. It is good enough if you spare me sadness wherever possible, and sweeten my life the way you do with your love (emphasis mine).

While in Dutta and Robinson, the same passage is rendered as:

> *To make me happy you need not try very hard – your sincere love is enough. Of course, if you and I could be united in everything we do and think, that would be best – but one cannot will such things [...] I do not want to leave you* behind *in anything – but at the same time I am afraid of forcing you. Each of us has his own separate taste, inclination and ability.* You do not possess the power to make your own nature correspond with my wishes and inclinations. *Therefore, instead of torturing yourself about it, if you sweeten my life with your love and care, and try to protect me from unnecessary pain, your efforts will be precious to me (my emphasis).*

Every translation is inevitably also an act of interpretation, but the two interpretations emerging from the above passages are pulling in two quite different directions. Telling your wife how much you value her love, hoping to transcend all separation and merge in both thought and action, while realizing that is unattainable, is quite different from telling you wife that she is incapable (*you do not posses the power*) of moulding herself to your expectations, so she need not *torture* herself about it, for inevitably she will be left *behind*, something you deeply regret. The interpretative thrust that guides Dutta and Robinson rests on their conviction that "while Rabindranath was certainly affectionate towards [Mrinalini], his feelings did not seem to have had the depth of genuine companionship". Elsewhere in their introduction the finality of their verdict is even more disparaging: "Rabindranath's simple affection for his young wife Mrinalini, and her lack of sophistication, are clear from this letter, written on board ship to Europe".

In contrast, Uma Das Gupta's reading evokes an altogether softer, more intimate, at times deeply touching, voice. "His letters tell us how closely he communicated with her, how much he wanted his family near him". If one interpretation places Tagore's young family "at the centre of his life", the other sees his family to have been an increasingly subordinate part of "the greater cause to which he felt his life was dedicated". Inadvertently, as with all translated texts, we find ourselves pondering how much of what we are reading is the actual voice of Tagore and how much the voice of the translator.

Where do the two successfully converge and where do they pull apart? The greatest challenge of any translation is in getting the author's voice to come across as authentically as possible in another language, and to resist the temptation of imposing one's own. It is an exercise in humility as much as in linguistic aptitude. Through his own trials as a translator of his own writings, Tagore came to understand the vital importance, as well as the difficulty, of achieving both.

Translation is clearly a sensitive issue. In the appositely titled *A Difficult Friendship; Letters of Edward Thompson and Rabindranath Tagore 1913 – 1940* it was the very question of translation that first drove a wedge between Tagore and the ex-Methodist missionary, historian, novelist and poet, who was also his first serious Western biographer. With its overt criticism of Tagore, Thompson's second biography brought their friendship to a near breaking point. Whether that criticism was justified is an issue that still animates discussion in "Tagore circles".

Edward Thompson (1886 – 1967) was born of Wesleyan Methodist missionary parents and spent his first six years in India. He was then taken to England by his parents, only to return at the age of 24, taking up a teaching post at Bankura College in southern Bengal. He learned Bengali well enough to be able to read and appreciate Tagore in the original. Entering Tagore's life at the crucial juncture of the poet receiving the Nobel Prize, when having English translations became a matter of increased urgency, Thompson, being a creative writer himself, was drawn into the intricate web of Tagore's many literary collaborators and associates.

He was a zealous participant, sometimes over-zealous, and Tagore, having risen in stature overnight and suddenly pulled into the vortex of public life, did not find it easy to cope with Thompson's eagerness to assist him. "When men thickly surround me and clamour for their dues", he wrote to Thompson in what must have been more than a subtle attempt to ward him off, "they do not get my best". Indeed, in this exchange Tagore reveals a side to his character that those who desire to see him as superhuman would prefer to ignore. There was certainly something of a prima donna in the way he would engage Thompson when it suited him and dismiss him when it did not.

The ins-and-outs of what came to pass between the poet, the translator-*cum*-proofreader circle of Tagore's English collaborators, and the Macmillan Company of London is minutely recorded and presented in another of Uma Das Gupta's sophisticated and scholarly books. All the surviving letters between the two men are arranged into eight chronologically arranged chapters and annotated with comprehensive notes. The book also has a substantial introduction covering the wider background to their relationship, as well as separate smaller introductions to the letter sections, providing further context and commentary to their exchange.

At times the commentary seems almost more interesting than the letters, which often deal with the practicalities of their working relationship, and are rather brusque and factual. Certainly they are not as engaging as the letters Tagore wrote to William Rothenstein or C. F. Andrews, his other two lifelong friends and associates. It was only towards the end of their difficult friendship, once they had both managed "to overcome national egoism, personal pain, and mutual annoyance" (Das Gupta's 2003: 2), and were able to share their ideas with understanding that their letters became more full-bodied. Tagore was able to appreciate more fully Thompson's "interest in international justice" and assimilate his harsh criticism of his own translations in a moment of painful self-realisation: "I have done gross injustice to my original productions partly owing to my incompetence and partly to carelessness". Thompson, on the other hand, gave Tagore all the recognition he deserved: "[Y]ou stand for a new kind of man, neither Eastern nor Western but a reconciler of the best of both".

While the two biographies are clearly aimed at a wide readership across the English-speaking world, *Difficult Friendship* is more specifically a Tagoreophile treat. It complements nicely earlier works dealing with this troublesome but ultimately fulfilling relationship across the colonial divide, especially E. P. Thompson's brilliant study of his father's relationship with the Bengali poet, aptly titled *Alien Homage.*

If there is an air of polemics surrounding this corner of Tagore studies (E. P. Thompson apart, we can mention also William Radice, Harish Trivedi, and Mary Lago), Uma Das Gupta chooses to steer away from these controversies. In her characteristic fashion she prefers to present the facts and let them speak for themselves.

• • •

3

The Sources of Tagore's Poetic Imagination

A reader conversant with the high points of ancient Sanskrit literature and medieval Bengali literature as well as English literature from Spenser to Swinburne on the one hand, and the monotheistic Upanishadic Hinduism and Christianity as practised in the 19th century (with its concomitant Puritanism) on the other, will realise that Tagore's poetic and lyrical imagination had three major aspects: devotion to the Upanishadic Brahman-formless, attributeless, yet all-pervasive; an abiding enchantment with nature, specifically the natural scenes of the lower Gangetic plains, richly varying through the cycle of the seasons; and last, but perhaps the most powerful - an intense yearning for romantic love. The informed Bengali reader can, with a little effort, trace the roots of the poetic style which he developed to the emotional need to express these and the influence of the literary sources cited above. Those who, like Rothenstein and Yeats did not have a close acquaintance with Classical Sanskrit literature and Bengali poetic literature from Kalidasa to Michael Madhusudan Dutt, inclusive of the Vaishnava poets, and the prose of Bankim Chandra Chatterjee are and were unlikely to be in a position to appreciate, even to a modest extent, the nuances of word, idiom and imagery which constitute the characteristic style of Tagore.

The Fundamental Confusion

The role that Vaishnava poetry played in Tagore's artistic development was formidable; one cannot do better than to quote him in this context: "If you ask what gave me boldness when I was young I should say that one thing was my early acquaintance with the old 'Vaishnava' poems of Bengal, full of freedom in meter and expression. I think I was only twelve when these poems first began to be reprinted.

I surreptitiously obtained copies from the desks of my elders. . . I must. . . admit that the greater part of these lyrics was erotic and not quite suited to a boy just about to reach his teens, but my imagination was completely occupied with the beauty of their forms and the music of their words and their breath, heavily laden with voluptuousness, passed over my mind without distracting it." To Yeats, Rothenstein, Pound and their associates, these origins of Tagore's poetic imagination and emotional life were largely unknown; it was, therefore, possible, and perhaps imperative, for them to accept him as a quasi-saint whose spiritual quests were aided rather than retarded by a tamely sentimental view of romantic love, in line with Christian morality.

Yet Vaishnava verses like their ancient Sanskrit predecessors, in their spirit, were the most un-Christian literary compositions conceivable Amiya Chakravarty, himselfa competent poet and Tagore's one-time literary secretary felt obliged to add the following words, in a note, with reference to the passage quoted above: "The erotic tendency of some Vaishnava poetry, especially in connection with degenerate forms of the cult of Radha and Krishna had aroused opposition among the more sober-minded Hindus." This must not be treated as an insignificant footnote; it refers, in fact to a problem which plagued Tagore throughout his life, which I shall now have to address.

Imbued as he was with the densely sensual spirit and imageries of Vaishnava poetry, yet embedded in the Puritanical educated elite of 19th century Bengal, the daunting dilemma that Tagore faced was that of creating a style for himself through which passionate romantic love could be portrayed in a sensitive, appealing and varied manner without offending the moral sensibilities of the age, which were formed in the main, by the general mood of the Bengal renaissance.

In the English romantic poets, Tagore found a world in which love and emotions directly or indirectly connected to it, were expressed in an entirely different idiom; one which in its exquisite poignancy and delight was in consonance with a more spiritual, and less corporeal conception of amorous relations than was to be met with in the ancient Sanskritic and the medieval Vaishnavite literature.

It has been affirmed or conjectured by Tagorean writers that Tagore created for himself a personal deity, whom he addressed by the second person singular. Yet his religious beliefs and indeed that of his father were based fundamentally on the Upanishadic Brahman who, being non-anthropomorphic, could not be addressed directly by human beings. But the Christian Almighty cast his influence on the monotheism of Brahmoism and being anthropomorphic could be addressed freely in song and poetry.

The synthesis or intermixture of these two entities resulted in a deity who was formless and not susceptible of idol worship, yet could be the object of devotional songs and poetry making liberal use of the crucial second person singular. In Tagore's imagination, a female beloved and a male deity often merged with each other. He composed some songs in such a manner as to leave room for dual interpretations. An example of this device is: *Tomaare-i kariaachhi jIbaner-o dhrubataaraa* ("It is you whom I have chosen as the pole-star guiding my life. . . ") which appears in the section of *Gitabitan* titled Romantic Love (*Prem*), yet is included in the collection of monotheistic devotional songs Brahma-sangit. Significantly, the neo-Hindu celibate monk and missionary Swami Vivekaananda used to sing this song, one of his favourites. Though the second person singular was originally meant to represent an amorous beloved, in the Swami's conception, it certainly referred to the deity, for effusions of romantic love were strongly inimical to the ascetic spirit of the monastic order to which he belonged.

It is not difficult to find a typical example of the converse device — romantic or even quasi-erotic imageries pervading a devotional song included in the section of the *Gitabitan* titled 'Worship'(*Puja*): It appears as Item 20 in *Gitanjali* : "On the day when the lotus bloomed, alas, my mind was straying, and I knew it not". Perhaps few readers are able to sing this song which, to my knowledge, has been commercially recorded by only one senior artiste: "*Yedin phuTlo kamal kichhu-i jaani naai*". If the Bengali reader surveys this song in its entirety, recalls or listens to at least one faithful rendition of it and if possible hums the tune, he or she will intuitively grasp the mood and will recognise an element of indirect, subtle and tempered sensuality in it. It must be noticed that there is no mention of the deity whatsoever in this song: the poet speaks of himself, a lotus recently bloomed and the wistfulness that it evokes in his mind.

Numerous other examples may be located to this interchangeability and intermingling of religious and romantic devotion, of deity and beloved. However, for many songs such an interchangeability was not possible, and an indiscriminate oscillation between the two could only impair their mood and appeal. But Tagore knew that sensuous imageries were likely to offend Euro-American moral sensibilities, and as we have seen in one example he scrupulously deleted all reference to the sense of touch and indeed, any allusion that might suggest or evoke un-Christian shades of sensuous emotions. To this matter I shall have to return later in the essay. The peculiar handling of the dilemma pervades the descriptions of the cycle of the seasons, too, which make their own contributions to the incomprehensibilty of Tagore's lyrics for Western readers.

The role played by climate in Tagore's songs, therefore, have now to be considered. Monsoon was Tagore's favourite; but this is a misleadingly simplistic statement. What permeated the majority of Tagore's songs on nature is specifically the monsoon in the lower Gangetic plains. I do not believe that inhabitants of, say, Punjab, Kashmir or Goa, not to speak of the Western world, could ever be able to appreciate the character of Tagore's musical treatment of the characteristic features of monsoon therein: the dense and lush foliage; the tumultuous thundershowers; the merging of forest, field, river and sky into a single continuum of watery mass; and the primordial drama of the rain-bearing clouds which, centuries ago, had provoked

Kalidasa to compose some of the most bewitchingly beautiful verse in Sanskrit literature. *Gitanjali* offers several lyrics based on scenes of monsoon. It must be kept in mind that moods of monsoon pervade large stretches in the *Gitabitan* and is not limited to the section titled Monsoon (*Barshhaa*).

Item 22 of *Gitanjali* is as follows : 'In the deep shadows of the rainy July, with secret steps, thou walkest, silent as night, eluding all watchers.' This is the translation of song no. 94 of the section of the *Gitabitan* titled Monsoon (p463): "*aaji sraaban ghana gahan mohe, gopan taba charan phele/nishaar mata, nIrab ohe, sabaar diThi e.Daye ele.*"

The Bengali reader, upon contrasting the original and the translation will discern a perceptible difference in mood and atmosphere: the original pertains to the natural scenes in the Bengal monsoon that we have discussed; the translation is constrained to deal with a rainy season that is geographically unspecified, for Tagore has to speak to an English-speaking readership that is widely dispersed over more than one continent. The Western reader is unable to fix his or her mind firmly to any specific set of experiences characteristic of some specific region: this inevitably impairs or hinders the imagination and blurs the impact of the lyric on the mind. The English romantic poets made allusions to natural scenes of England which, however, were better known to readers in the Westernized parts of the Orient, especially, educated Indians, since through a formidable literature read and assimilated in early life, an indirect familiarity with English scenes had been accomplished.

But a discrepancy that is far more serious is one that is so subtle as to almost elude notice : the second person singular in the original is, as usual, a beloved; or else, the song would have been placed in the section of the *Gitabitan* titled 'Worship' (*Puja*). The word *helaa* (neglect or indifference) has been repeatedly used in the love songs of *Gitabitan* to describe an attitude particularly excruciating for the forlorn yearner after love. The last line of the original is "*samukh diye swapanasama jeyo naa more helaay Thele*"; in the translation one finds "do not pass by like a dream". The last two words "*helaay Thele*" (neglectfully evade or dismiss) have been expunged. Why? In the English translation the beloved of the original had had to be transformed or transmuted into a rather vaguely delineated entity, formed perhaps partially upon a personification of the deity: and a benevolent godhead is not supposed to forsake or neglect human beings in the manner in which a beloved might his or her lover. The poignant yearning expressed in the last line of the original is therefore enfeebled in the semi-devotionalised translation. The confusion is repeated in the next item (no. 23) of the *Gitanjali* :

> *"Art thou abroad on this stormy night on thy journey of love, my friend?"*
>
> *"Aaji jha.Der raate tomaar abhisaar paraansakhaa bandhu he aamaar/"*

The relatively innocent 'journey of love' represents *abhisaara* - the clandestine nocturnal prowl or jaunt of the lover who has a tryst with his beloved. Comparison of the last stanzas of the original and the translation shows a distinct alteration of the mood; for, though in the union of love there is uncertainty, in the communion with the deity, given sufficient devotion, there is none. Once again, Tagore had veered from his original mood, with the tastes of the West uppermost in his mind.

In his songs, Tagore often alluded to things more easily palpable, and when he set himself the task of translating them, he had to resort to devices even more disruptive than we have hitherto discussed, as the following citation illustrates: (Item 74, *Gitanjali*)

> *"The day is no more, the shadow is upon the earth. It is time I go to the stream to fill my pitcher." This is song No. 84,* Gitabitan*, p. 306 "Aar naa-i re belaa naamlo chhaayaa dharanite/Ebaar chal re ghaaTe kalaskhaani bhare nite".*

In the second stanza of the translation, we find "In the lonely lane there is no passerby, the wind is up, the ripples are rampant in the river."

The Bengali original: "*Ekhan bijan pathe kare naa keu aasa-jaaoyaa, ore, premnadite uThechhe Dheu, utal haaoyaa.*"

Premnadi (literally, river of love) has been translated as merely 'river'. Unbeknownst to many this song is based upon an old feature of rural Bengali society (for these observations I am indebted to the late Nirad C. Chaudhuri). When family women went to the adjoining river or pond to fill their pitchers, there often prowled by the wayside, and near the *ghats*, prospective or performing paramours waiting for a meeting with them. Few would fail to guess what such meetings resulted in. So irresistible was the appeal of such practices that folklore had received their imprint, social censure notwithstanding and Tagore had made a delicately nuanced and discreetly indirect reference to it in this song to create a pall of vague and languid amorousness hanging in the evening air. But in the English translation he had to alter the mood to make it suit Western moral demands; hence, river of love (figuratively, the emotion of love envisioned as a river, susceptible to ripples and waves) had to be curtailed to mere 'river'.

From the discussion above, there is no room for doubt as to who the last sentence of the song refers to : "There at the fording in the little boat the unknown man plays upon his lute." The Bengali original obviously belongs to the section of the *Gitabitan* titled Romantic Love (*Prem*).

Yet Yeats takes an unwarranted religious view of the item: ". . . a man sitting in a boat upon a river river playing upon a lute, . . . is God Himself!" And the misapprehension was not rectified by Tagore, perhaps understandingly.

Another curious contrast is also in line with our present theme: use of the word '*maayaa*' in its Sanskrit form, untranslated into English, (in item #71, *Gitanjali*), yet the ommission of the word "*leelaa*" and substitution of the word "pleasure" in its place (item #1 "Thou hast made me endless, such is thy pleasure" - "*Aamaare tumi asheshh korechho, emani leelaa taba*").

The word '*maayaa*' is spiritual, or even mystical, and free of erotic connotations; therefore it was left unstranslated; but "*leelaa*", referring to the playful dalliance of Lord Krishna with the voluptuous cowherd girls, had to be sanitized by the disappointing and misleading translation "pleasure".

A similar analysis of several other songs of *Gitanjali*, on similar lines, can be carried out by any Bengali reader who is conversant with the Bengali originals. I believe I have given enough examples to show that Tagore's poetic and lyrical imagination had foundations which often bordered on the voluptuary, and in this his spirit was moved by ancient Sanskrit verse and especially *Vaishnava* poetry, in which his mind had been steeped from early adolescence onward.

The songs of *Gitabitan* on love and nature have virtually nothing to do with the Christian model of piety and asceticism and Yeats's projection of Tagore as primarily a religious poet in the Christian mould was almost entirely erroneous. It is in vain that he alludes to the writing of European saints of the Renaissance in his discussion of Tagore's lyrics.

It is here that all the major shortcomings of *Gitanjali* lie, rather than in such faulty, and sometimes risible, translations such as "I sit like a beggar maid, drawing my skirt over my face, . . . ". An unnecessary and unfair amount of censure has been heaped on Tagore for literal faults in translations.

Unfortunately, so urgently eager was Tagore on entering the Western world of letters, that he made no effort to rectify Yeats's misconceptions; Tagore himself could have persuaded Yeats to be less sentimentally effusive and more realistic and true to the actual spirit of his songs in his Introduction to the *Gitanjali*; he did not. In this, intellectually if not morally, he was in error. Though Yeats's cloyingly laudatory introduction induced the West to take *Gitanjali* very seriously, at least initially, in the end it was this error which made an incurable confusion of ideas the basis of Tagore's image in the West.

Religion

If there is one word that can describe Tagore's principal capital when he proceeded to the West, it is 'religion'. It is finally as a religious missionary that the West accepted him.

Even his first patrons were struck by the religious spirit of his poetry : Sturge Moore wrote to a friend: "Yeats and Rothenstein had a Bengalee poet on view during the last days I was in London. I was first privileged to see him in Yeats's rooms and then to hear a translation of his poems made by himself and read by Yeats in Rothenstein's drawing room. His unique subject is 'the love of God'. When I told Yeats that I found his poetry preposterously optimistic he said "Ah, you see, he is absorbed in God."

But religion in Europe and America meant Christianity; and we have seen how Tagore had tailored and doctored the mood of his lyrics and poems to suit Christian expectations.

To be sure, Christianity was very much on his mind when he embarked upon his voyage to Europe in 1912. In his address to the inmates of his school at *Santiniketan* titled "On the Eve of Departure", he said:

> *"There is no dearth in Europe of heroic souls who stand firmly against th tyranny of the mighty. Such upright men do not hesitate to take sides with alien peoples in far-off lands and suffer in their account. Who indeed are the friends of the Indians seeking self-government for their country ?. . . They are the knights who have undertaken to defend the weak. They tread in the hard path of Christ, stained with the blood of the divine leader who took the sorrows of the world upon himself to save the soul of man and to lead him from darkness into light. Deep within the heart of Europe that light still shines."*

One can clearly notice that his interest in Christianity was intimately bound-up with nationalistic political considerations.

He wrote: 'Many have asked me, "Why do you want to travel in Europe?" and he remarked in this address, "I have not known how to answer them."' The rest of the address is a long-winded justification of his voyage; but nowhere does he say that his interests were literary; poetry is not discussed.

One might begin to suspect that his journey to Europe and his publication of the English *Gitanjali* constituted the first deliberate step towards acquiring a Western image which would provide him with a political standing in the emerging nation. Without Western recognition, he realised, the whole of India would never take seriously the political views of one who was a mere poet confined to the cultural milieu of Bengal. It was Yeats's fulsome Introduction to the English *Gitanjali* that set the stage for the emergence of Tagore as a religious prophet in the West, very much in the Christian mould. He observes, "Since the Renaissance the writing of European saints—however familiar their metaphor and the general structure of their thought — has ceased to hold our attention. He goes on to mention St. Bernard, the Book of Revelation, a Kempis, John of the Cross and St. Francis in his Introduction.

And very significantly, Yeats observes, ". . . yet we are not moved because of its strangeness, but because we have met our own image, . . . "

Gradually, a notion developed in the West that his verse demonstrates that Christianity had permeated the lives of millions in India, thus Westernizing it religiously; and that he was at the vanguard of this conversion. Harriet Monroe, in whose residence in Chicago Tagore spent a few weeks, in her memoirs described *Gitanjali* as "those sacred songs of praise which were chanted everywhere in his native India."

That certain sections of the Christian establishment too held a similar view is shown by the following citation from the Baptist Times, February 2, 1914 :

> *"The poems of Rabindranath Tagore are valuable for their performance, but still more valuable for the promise they afford of a coming dawn. We have been waiting anxiously for some indication of the effect of Christian ideas on a truly representative Hindu mind. Here, surely, is the person we have been longing for — one sent before the chariot of the Lord to make His path straight. And when we remember that this poet's every word is eagerly caught up by waiting millions, may we venture to assert that the new, the Christian India, is already at the door?"*

The Christian India, however, is yet to emerge.

Later Reactions

I have now to deal with the later reactions to Tagore's work in the West. Ezra Pound, one of the coterie of poets who first championed Tagore in the West, later bitterly rejected Tagore's religious themes purveyed to the West through poetry. Romain Rolland, too, was critical of Tagore's preaching tours. Greene, the ruthless realist, remarked in 1937: "As for Rabindranath Tagore, I cannot believe that anyone but Mr. Yeats can still take his poems very seriously." (He was, of course, referring to the West.) But already in 1935, even this last eminent admirer of Tagore had lost his patience with him: an irritated Yeats thundered in a letter to Rothenstein in 1935 : "Damn Tagore. We got out three good books, Sturge Moore and I, and then, because he thought it more important to see and know English than to be a great poet, he brought out sentimental rubbish and wrecked his reputation. Tagore does not know English, no Indian knows English. Nobody can write with music and style in a language not learned in childhood and ever since the language of his thought."

The works of Nirad C. Chaudhuri and R. K. Narayan have conclusively disproved the misguided verdict: ". . . no Indian knows English. "Yet Yeats's annoyance with Tagore has to be accorded the attention that it deserves. It is amusing to observe the contrast of this quotation and the fulsome introduction to the *Gitanjali*.

Unfortunately, the honest and starkly expressed observations of a fair number of eminent intellectuals of the West in respect of Tagore were made in private correspondences which have been published much after the initial Western ballyhoo about Tagore. D. H Lawrence saw the unreal nature of the prevailing Western attitude towards Tagore, based on ignorance of the East, and wrote to Russell's mistress Lady Ottoline Morrell in May 1916: ". . . this fraud of looking up to them—this wretched worship-of-Tagore attitude—is disgusting."

Harsh words. But true, unfortunately.

Bertrand Russell was even more trenchant in his appraisal of Tagore the lecturing spiritualist. In a letter to Lady Ottoline, dated June 19, 1913, he wrote: "Here I am back from Tagore's lecture, after walking most of the way home. It was unmitigated rubbish - cut-and-dried conventional stuff about the river becoming one with the ocean and man becoming one with *Brahma*. . . "

Later, when asked his opinion of a letter Tagore wrote him on the essence of religion, he curtly wrote; ". . . His talk about the infinite is vague nonsense. The sort of language that is admired by many Indians unfortunately does not, in fact, mean anything at all." My heart goes out to those disciples of Tagore who are hurt by these sincere yet strong words of Russell; but I know too much about Russell to be able to dismiss this assertion as one based on incomprehension.

It becomes evident, then, that quite a few Western intellectuals could see through the essential unreality of Tagore's Western image; yet the private expressions of their perceptions did not become known publicly during Tagore's lifetime, perhaps mercifully. But the tragedy is that Tagore was at his highest in his songs, especially the descriptive ones, based on natural scenes and the cycle of the seasons, and it is precisely his music to which the West is necessarily deaf. It is in his songs of nature and love that Tagore expresses his true sensual self, which he felt compelled in the last decade of his life to express to a large extent in a rather unusual manner in his paintings.

Prose and Paintings

Tagore's novels and other prose works enjoyed a transient reputation in the West. His play 'The Post Office' was widely appreciated; and surprisingly, the anthologies of his works that have been published so far contain more prose than poetry. His lectures and letters do not present the difficulties of translations that his poetry and songs do, and this is one reason they feature profusely in these collections. Tagore remarked in 1930, 'My poetry is for my countrymen, my paintings are my gift to the West.

'His latest biographers state, "The best of the paintings— several hundred — are powerfully appealing (and suggestive of the untranslatable delicacies in the poetry.)". Actually, his paintings were a rather belated outlet for feelings which he could never clearly express in his songs and poetry, given the limitations of the style which he assumed rather early in life. There is a pagan element in some of them, which set them apart from all his verbal creations. However, the greater part of Tagore's Western image is based on his poems and lyrics, and had become fixed within a decade of the publication of *'Gitanjali.'*

Politics and Nationalism

Once Tagore acquired an image in the West, those in Bengal who were previously censorious of his work suddenly began to hold him in esteem, leaders such as Gandhi sought his comradeship. He had achieved his objective. Thereby he quickly acquired a nationalistic image which held sway all over India, and eventually he allowed himself to be viewed as a religio-political leader of a stature almost comparable to Gandhi. This image, which had its origins in his Western image, further reinforced the latter, through nationalistic propaganda. All major Indian political leaders felt called upon to comment on his life and work; of these judgments we examine only the most salient, made by the most eminent.

Dr. Sarvepalli Radhakrishnan who, being a Tamil, did not possess a knowledge of Tagore's work comparable to that possessed by any ordinary educated Bengali, summarised Tagore's oeuvre as follows:

> *"In all Rabindranath's work three features are striking : (1) The ultimateness of spiritual values to be obtained by inward honesty and cultivation of inner life; (2) the futility of mere negation or renunciation and the need for a holy or a whole development of life; and (3) the positive attitude of sympathy for all, even the lowly and the lost. It is a matter for satisfaction to find an Indian leader insisting on these real values of life at a time when so many old things are crumbling away and a thousand new ones are springing up."*

This verdict almost defies comment; so vast is its scope, and so vague is the sense in which the words have been used, that one might employ this very summary in characterising the work not of Tagore but of any one amongst Gandhi, Vivekananda and Aurobindo Ghose. No Westerner, who has not read Tagore, can guess from this statement that he was primarily a composer of Bengali songs and poetry.

Jawaharlal Nehru's judgment is, of course, frankly political, and he too was unable to read even a single page of *Gitabitaan* in the original Bengali : ". . . Rabindranath Tagore has given to our nationalism the outlook of internationalism and has enriched it with art and music and the magic of his words, so that it has become the full-blooded emblem of INDIA'S awakened spirit." (Emphasis mine)

Perhaps Nehru the intellectual (as opposed to the politician) had the perspicacity to see, though he found it imprudent to state, that it was far easier for Tagore to reach out to the Bengali-speaking people of (the erstwhile) East Pakistan through his songs and thereby become an emblem, whether full-blooded or not, of its awakening spirit, which was to lead to the creation of Bangladesh merely seven years after his decease, than to enthrall entire populations of the speakers of Tamil, Telugu, Kannada, Malayalam, Marathi, Gujarati et al who, knowing no Bengali, had no access to his songs and poetry at all. And Gandhi proclaimed, "I regard the poet as a sentinel warning us against the approach of enemies called Bigotry, Lethargy, Intolerance, Ignorance, Inertia and other memebers of that brood."

From all this emerges an image of a religio-political leader, always on the road, addressing hortatory speeches and sermons to great masses of people; its superficiality can be seen by any educated Bengali. But if such be the utterances of non-Bengali Indians who, on account of their exalted political positions, were naturally taken seriously in the West, one can hardly blame Westerners alone for creating a grandiosely false image of Tagore.

The Man Himself

An author who has made bold to claim that the Western image of Tagore is ersatz will perhaps be expected to set forth an account of his true identity, undistorted and unaberrated.

The fact of the matter, unfortunately, is that Tagore's temperament was essentially unsuited to an active public or political life; he was fundamentally a loner whose creative energies found their ideal expression in solitude.

Though he was aggressively litigious - he had been engaged in furious lawsuits over property with several of his siblings (inclusive of his once-beloved Jyotirindranath) and even when on his deathbed in 1941, was involved in a legal battle with his only surviving sibling Barnakumari (who was at that time about 90) - he was not emotionally equipped to withstand the wear and tear of public censure and ridicule to which every politician and active public person is inevitably subject; poets seldom are.

Here I must let the man speak for himself. When he was thirty-one, he wrote: "Intimacy with men is absolutley intolerable to me. Unless I have plenty of room around myself I cannot stretch my limbs, settle down and unpack my mind. I pray that mankind may prosper, but they should not jostle me. . . " Again, when he was thirty-two he wrote, speaking of his mind: "It is only when it gets a little solitude that it can muse to its heart's content, look round itself, and express its feelings in all their meanderings exactly as it pleases."

Chaudhuri rightly states, "It is from this Tagore that his greatest literary achievement came out. He is at his greatest as a writer when he is speaking as a lone soul with a lone voice to lone souls."

As for romantic love, the exultant eroticism of ancient and medieval Sanskrit literature provided him with imageries, but the mood of his songs of love are often, if not always, of sorrow and despair. Throughout his life he yearned in vain for an idealised form of romantic love, and this failure caused him intense anguish till his last days. His songs express it in a delicate manner with which many Bengalis, similarly deprived, can identify their feelings.

Out of a plethora of songs as examples, I choose only one:

"You are indeed my heart's desire,

I have nothing and no one in this world except you.

I shall lose myself in my separation from you, and thereby live in you
Through long days, long nights, long months, and long years.
If you love someone else, and never come back,
May you get all that you seek,
And I bear all the sorrow that there may be. "

But it was his profound love of nature that enabled him to save his soul. Once again, we must let the man speak for himself:

"I feel that once upon a time I was at one with the rest of the earth, that grass grew green upon me, that the autumn sun fell on me and under its rays the warm scent of youth wafted from every pore of my far-flung evergreen body. As my waters and mountains lay spread out through every land, dumbly soaking up the radiance of a cloudless sky, an elixir of life and joy was inarticulately secreted from the immensity of my being. So it is that my feelings seem to be those of our ancient planet, ever germinant and efflorescent, shuddering with sun-kissed delight. The current of my consciousness streams through each blade of grass, each sucking root, each sappy vein, and breaks out in the waving fields of corn and in the rustling leaves of the palms."

One man, his solitude, his yearnings for love, and his love of nature — all experienced and expressed through a highly sensuous musical and poetic intuition : this is the essential Tagore.

Conclusion

That his image in the West was a brittle fabric of appreciation based on incomprehension had of course become clear to him, if it had not been evident right from the beginning. But the very Bengalis whose harsh censure and ridicule had pained him and against whom he had hit out time and again were not susceptible to the misinterpretations to which the West was prone; the Bengalis sang his songs spontaneously and with genuine passion, in celebration of the seasons, of love and even of religion. Inasmuch as he had been at perfect harmony with Bengal, its rivers, verdant fields and villages, his songs, especially the seasonal ones, had an enduring character free from all temporary literary or religious fads and fashions, and consequently merged with the life of the Bengali mind completely. He remarked in his last days that the fate of his poems and stories was uncertain, but his songs had indeed found a lasting lodgment in the hearts of Bengalis.

Bengal, in the end, was his true home, as it had been at the dawn of his life. But what did the West gain from him? I shall have to quote Alex Aronson :

> *"A great scholar would expound the philosophy of Rabindranath in terms of metaphysics and mysticism; a politician would elucidate his position in European politics; litterateurs would establish comparisons and parallels; and priests of various denominations would exalt or debase his spiritual message. Everyone of them had his own axe to grind, and Rabindranath became a useful and innocent tool which they knew how to handle for their own ulterior purposes.*
>
> *So it came about that he was unknowingly made to represent certain tendencies in the party-politics of various nations, that his name was freely used for the sake of either appeasing or inflaming national hatred, and that the various religious or pseudo-racial denominations used him for their own ends. The litterateurs were often uncritical and outrageously condescending. In addition to all this an atmosphere of sensationalism was being created around him symptomatic of the loss of mental equilibrium, and perhaps also of the loss of all beliefs in the West."*
>
> *". . . Rabindranaths's voice when it was heard in Europe evoked (in Mathew arnold's words about Shelley) "a vision of beauty and radiance, indeed, but availing nothing, effecting nothing."*

Indeed, now that we approach the centenary of Tagore's first encounter with the West, and find feeble voices still shrieking in order to continue projecting an ersatz Western image of the poet based on incomprehension and academic sensationalism, what profound religious faith, what luminous truth about humanity, is being upheld by his Western champions?

We might well wonder.

The Year 1400

A hundred years from today who are you, sitting, reading a poem of mine, under curiosity's sway - a hundred years from today?

Not the least portion of this young spring's morning bliss, neither blossom nor birdsong, nor any of its scarlet splashes can I drench in passion and despatch to your hands a hundred years hence! Yet do this, please: unlatch your south-faced door, just sit at your window for once; basking in fantasy, eyes on the far horizon, figure out if you can: how one day a hundred years back roving delights in a free fall from a heavenly region had touched all that there was-the infant Phalgun day, utterly free, was frenzied, all agog, while borne on brisk wings, the south wind pollen-scent-brushed had suddenly arrived and in a flash dyed the earth with all youth's hues a hundred years before your day.

There lived then a poet, ebullient of spirit, his heart steeped in song, who wanted to open his words like so many flowers with so much passion one day a hundred years back. A hundred years from today who is the new poet whose songs flow through your homes?

To him I convey this springtime's gladsome greetings.

May my vernal song find its echo for a moment in your spring day in the throbbing of your hearts, in the buzzing of your bees, in the rustling of your leaves a hundred years from today.

●●●

4

Rabindra Sangeet

Rabindrasangeet refers to a complete body of songs (approximately 2,230) and lyrical poetry written and composed by Bengali Nobel-laureate poet Rabindranath Tagore. The term refers to both the genre and the individual songs themselves.

Influence and Legacy

These songs are regarded as cultural treasures of Bengal in both Bangladesh and West Bengal (India).

The *Rabindrasangeet*, which deal with varied themes are immensely popular and form a foundation for the Bengali ethos that is comparable to, perhaps even greater than, that which Shakespeare has on the English-speaking world. It is said that his songs are the outcome of 500 years of literary & cultural churning that the Bengali community has gone through.

In his book *Caste and Outcaste*, Dhan Gopal Mukerji has said that these songs transcend the mundane to the aesthetic and express all ranges and categories of human emotion. The poet had given a voice to all—big or small, rich or poor. The poorest boatman on the Ganges as well as the rich landlord find expression for their emotional trials and tribulations in Tagore's songs.

Rabindrasangeet has evolved into a distinctive school of music. Practitioners of this genre are known to be fiercely protective of tradionalist practice. Novel interpretations and variations have drawn severe censure in both West Bengal and Bangladesh. And like Beethoven's symphonies or Vilayat Khan's sitar, Rabindrasangeet demands an educated, intelligent & cultured audience to appreciate the lyrical beauty of his compositions.

He was among the first to recognize that cinema should have its own language. In 1929 he wrote, "The beauty and grandeur of this form in motion has to be developed in such a way that it becomes self-sufficient without the use of words." The inherent beauty & depth of Tagore's songs have persuaded a number of filmmakers to use Tagore's songs in their films including Satyajit Ray, Ritwik Ghatak, Mrinal Sen, Nitin Bose, Tapan Sinha and Kumar Shahani. His songs were also used in British, European & Australian movies just to capture the mood of a cinematic situation & to reveal a delicate interplay of relationships.

Ritwik Ghatak said of Tagore, "That man has culled all my feelings from long before my birth...I read him and find that...I have nothing new to say." In his *Meghe Dhaka Tara* (The Cloud-capped Star) and *Subarnarekha*, Ghatak uses *Rabindrasangeet* to express the poignancy of post-Partition Bengal. Two of the songs written by Tagore are the national anthems of India and Bangladesh. These are:

- Bangladesh: "*Amar Shonar Bangla*"
- India: "*Jana Gana Mana*"

Singers of *Rabindrasangeet*

Some of the well-known singers of *Rabindrasangeet* are:

- Pankaj Mullick also known as the *First Man* of Rabindrasangeet.
- Hemanta Kumar Mukhopadhyay
- Debabrata Biswas also known as the *Second Man* of Rabindrasangeet & unarguably the most popular among male voices.
- Subinoy Roy.
- Kanika Bandyopadhyay her original name was "Anima" but Tagore had renamed her "Kanika" and Abanindranath Tagore used to call her *Mohar* by which name she is known to many of her dedicated listeners.

- Suchitra Mitra
- Rajeshwari Dutta was originally from Punjab. She was married to a well-known Bengali poet, Sudhindranath Dutta. She made her mark in the classical-based *tappa* and other compositions
- Argha Sen
- Ashoketaru Bandyopadhyay
- Beethin Bandopadhyay
- Banani Ghosh
- Dwijen Mukhopadhay
- Chinmay Chattopadhyay
- Gita Ghatak
- Iffatara Khan
- Mita Huq
- Nilima Sen
- Promita Mollik
- Purba Dam
- Rajasree
- Rajeswari Dutta
- Rezwana Chowdhury Banya
- Ritu Guha
- Roma Mondal
- Rono Gohathakurota
- Ruma Guha Thakurta
- Sadi Mohammad
- Sagar Sen
- Sumitra Sen
- Sanghamitramitra Gupta
- Susil Mullick
- Swagatalakshmi Dasgupta
- swapan Gupta
- Ashok Das
- Monica Ghose
- Sasha A.K. Ghoshal

Teachers of *Rabindrasangeet*

Some of the well-known teachers of Rabindrasangeet (barring Tagore himself) are:

- Dinendra Nath Tagore
- Shantideb Ghosh
- Ashoketaru Bandyopadhyay
- Dwijen Mukhopadhay
- Shailaja Ranjan Majumdar
- Maya Sen
- Suchitra Mitra
- Rajasree
- Kanika Bandyopadhyay
- Rezwana Chowdhury Banya
- Subinoy Roy
- Swagatalakshmi Dasgupta

In Bangladesh, prominent Rabindrasangeet trainers who have contributed immensely in developing new artistes include :

- Sanjida Khatun
- Wahidul Haq deceased
- Ajit Ray
- Anisur Rahman
- Papia Sarwar
- Lily Islam
- Rezwana Chowdhury Banya
- Selina Malek
- Mita Haq
- Sadi Mohammad
- Fazle Nizami deceased
- Hamida Haq
- Atiqul Islamdeceased
- Chanchal Khan (In Australia now)
- Kaderi Kibria (In USA)
- Sirajus Salekin (In Australia)

- Rakhi Chakravarti (Overseas)
- Salma Akhbar
- Tapan Mahmud
- Bulbul Islam
- Mahadev Shaha
- Shahjahan Kamal Taught at Jhankar Academy, Bongio Sankskritic Chakra (Dhaka), Presently teaching at Alampia School of Music (Toronto).

Ekla Chalo Re

Jodi Tor Dak Shune Keu Na Ashe is a song written by Rabindranath Tagore, part of the Rabindra Sangeet canon. It exhorts the listener to continue his or her journey, despite abandonment or lack of support from others. The song is often quoted in the context of political or social change movements; Mahatma Gandhi cited it as one his favourite songs.

Lyrics

In Bengali Script

যদি তার ডাক শুনে কউ না আসে তবে একলা চলো র।
একলা চলো, একলা চলো, একলা চলো, একলা চলো র

যদি কউ কথা না ক , ওরে ওরে ও অভাগা,
যদি সবাই থাকে মুখ ফিরা সবাই করে ভ ---
তবে পরান খুলে
ও তুই মুখ ফুটে তার মনের কথা একলা বলো র

যদি সবাই ফিরে যা , ওরে ওরে ও অভাগা,
যদি গহন পথে যাবার কালে কউ ফিরে না চা ---
তবে পথের কাঁটা
ও তুই র মাথা চরণতলে একলা দলো র

যদি আলো না ধরে, ওরে ওরে ও অভাগা,
যদি ঝ -বাদলে আঁধার রাতে দু ার দ ঘরে---
তবে ব ানলে
আপন বুকের পাঁজর ালি নি একলা লো র

In Bengali Romanization

Jodi tor ðak shune keu na ashe tôbe êkla chôlo re,
Êkla chôlo, êkla chôlo, êkla chôlo, êkla chôlo re.
Jodi keu kôtha na kôe, ore ore o ôbhaga,
Jodi shôbai thake mukh firaee shôbai kôre bhôe—
Tôbe pôran khule
O tui mukh fuþe tor moner kôtha êkla bôlo re.
Jodi shôbai fire jae, ore ore o ôbhaga,
Jodi gôhon pôthe jabar kale keu fire na chae—
Tôbe pôther kãþa
O tui rôktomakha chôrontôle êkla dôlo re.
Jodi alo na dhôre, ore ore o ôbhaga,
Jodi jhôº-badole ãdhar rate duar dêe ghôre—
Tôbe bojranôle
Apon buker pãjor jalie nie êkla jôlo re.

Tagore's English Translation

If they answer not to thy call walk alone,

If they are afraid and cower mutely facing the wall,

O thou of evil luck, open thy mind and speak out alone.

If they turn away, and desert you when crossing the wilderness,

O thou of evil luck, trample the thorns under thy tread, and along the blood-lined track travel alone.

If they do not hold up the light when the night is troubled with storm,

O thou of evil luck, with the thunder flame of pain ignite thy own heart and let it burn alone.

In Popular Culture

- The song was used in the 2005 film Netaji Subhas Chandra Bose: The Forgotten Hero
- "Ekla Chalo Re" is the title of a book by the Jain Acharya Mahaprajna

- The song was famously sung by Vinoba Bhave during the beginnings of his Bhoodan movement, with "blessed" substituted for "unfortunate".

Tagore Songs unique treasure of Rabindranath's creative life. Opinions differ on when he first started composing songs. According to some authorities, his first song was composed when he was 12; some others say he began composing songs in 1875 at the age of 14. He then composed 'Jval jval chita dvigun dvigun' for the play *Sarojini* written by his elder brother JYOTIRINDRANATH TAGORE. The same year two songs by him appeared in print as offerings for HINDU MELA. One of them, 'Tomari tare ma sanpinu e deha' (O mother, this body of mine is dedicated to you), was undisputedly composed by Tagore; but the other, 'Ek sutre bandhiyachhi sahasrati man' (I have tied a thousand minds with one string), is regarded by some as having been composed or set to music by Jyotirindranath Tagore. If 'Tomari tare ma ...' was composed at the age of 12, it was certainly Tagore's first song. For his last birthday he composed 'He nutan, dekha dik ar-bar janmer pratham shubhaksan' (Hail the new, let the auspicious moment of birth appear again) on 7 May 1941. This means he composed songs for 68 years. All his 2,232 songs have been compiled in his *Gitabitan*.

The tradition of pre-Rabindranath Bangla songs took a new turn in the Tagore family. Rabindranath's father DEBENDRANATH TAGORE, brothers SATYENDRANATH TAGORE and Jyotirindranath Tagore and others composed a genre of devotional songs for Brahma Samaj prayers. In this respect they were following RAMMOHUN ROY. Rabindranath enriched the genre by following his brothers in composing Brahma Sangit in the classical style.

Tagore songs are deeply influenced by classical influence. Although he himself did not learn CLASSICAL MUSIC formally, the family atmosphere of cultivating this form of music enables him to compose many of his songs in the Hindustani classical style. On the occasion of Brahmo Samaj's *Magh* festival, he composed many devotional songs in the Hindustani classical style. The Tagore songs composed in this tradition are treasures of our music. Many of his songs abound in the classical forms of *sthayi*, *antara*, *sanchari* and *abhog*. The influence of the classical style is also manifested in the tunes, words and articulation of the songs. During his childhood, several music teachers from the Vishnupur gharana used to come to the Tagore house. Of them, Vishnuchandra Chakravarty and Radhikaprasad Goswami left a deep impression on Tagore's mind. The RAGAS and *raginis* heard in his childhood managed to cast long shadows on his songs.

Rabindranath established his uniqueness by applying multiple ragas and raginis in a single song. For instance, he applied four ragas - *lalit*, *vibhas*, *jogiya* and *ashavari* - in his song 'Achhe duhkha achhe mrtyu, biraha dahana lage'. To him, theme was more important than ragas. Even in folk tunes he experimented with a mixture of ragas to create a genre of his own. TAPPA is yet another form that has enriched Tagore songs. The use of tappa in giving expression to Bengali emotions has been noteworthy. Rabindranath composed some songs following the tappa tradition of 'Shori Miar Punjabi'. His own tappas utilize no discernible combination of TALS. The use of folk tunes is also obvious in Tagore tappas.

Rabindranath composed tunes for some Vedic and Bauddha hymns to create devotional songs. He also composed a number of songs with the help of South Indian tunes. The folksongs of Bengal have significantly influenced Tagore songs too. He used extensively tunes and styles from BAUL, KIRTAN, shyamasangit, *sari* and even *kathakata* to give his songs a distinctive flavour and beauty.

Rabindranath's familiarity with the folk tunes, and kirtan, syamasangit and ramprasadi is seen in the songs he composed between 1884 and 1886. The use of baul tunes became noticeable since 1905. While agitating against the PARTITION OF BENGAL, Rabindranath realized that the best way to touch the hearts of the people was to utilize the tunes drawn from the soil. Twenty songs composed by him at the time were published in a book entitled *Baul*. Among them were Gandhiji's favourite song 'Yadi tor dak shune keu na ase tabe ekla chalo re' (If no one comes to respond to your call, go forth all alone) and 'Amar sonar Bangla, ami tomay bhalobasi' (My Bengal of gold, I love you), later adopted as the NATIONAL ANTHEM of Bangladesh. Rabindranath also used folk tunes from different Indian states like Mumbai, Gujarat, Madras, Mysore and Punjab (Sikh bhajan).

The Tagore family was familiar with many western musical tunes. In his AUTOBIOGRAPHY, Rabindranath speaks of a book called *Irish Melodies* that he read early in life. His grandfather DWARAKANATH TAGORE was known to have taken lessons in western music. The family of Rabindranath's elder brother Satyendranath Tagore used to cultivate western music. His knowledge about western music was enhanced when at the age of 17 he went to England to study bar-at-law and had an opportunity to live with different English families. He applied many western tunes in the songs of his musical plays *Valmiki Pratibha* (1881) and *Kalmrgaya* (1882). Thanks to his unique abilities, he could maintain his own distinctive note even after using varied elements from other musical sources. Because of this quality, his tunes can be easily identified even when he has based them on other musical forms.

Rabindranath has used many tals in composing songs. These included *chautal*, *ada chautal*, *dhamar*, *adatheka*, *surfankta*, *yat*, *jhanptal*, *trital*, *ektal*, *teoda*, *dadra*, *kaharba* and *adkhemta*. He has utilized some tals which are new to North Indian music; these include *sasthi*, *jhampak*, *rupkada*, *navatal*, *ekadashi* and *navapanchatal*. In poetic measures too, Rabindranath showed some distinctiveness, especially in using multiple times. He has occasionally used multiple tempos in a single song and has skillfully mixed times and tempos to create a very unusual musical form.

Usually songs have a preponderance of tunes and measures but Tagore songs are essentially poetic and therefore their poetic themes are as important as their tunes. The thematic variety of his songs reflects the rich emotional life of Bengalis. *Gitabitan*, his main and final compilation of songs, has a large number of sections. His devotional songs have been listed under 'Puja', love songs under 'Prem', songs on seasons under 'Prakrti', patriotic songs under 'Swadesh', occasional songs under 'Anusthanik', and miscellaneous songs under 'Vichitra'.

Some of his songs for his stage plays are satirical. The divisions of his songs relating to worship, love and nature are no doubt arbitrary as the themes are often intermixed so overwhelmingly that drawing clear lines between them becomes difficult.

His occasional songs treat an amazing variety of themes. He wrote songs on weddings, births and deaths, house warming, tree planting, plowing land, sinking a tubewell, tying rakhi, convocations, inauguration ceremonies, harvesting and even teaching of martial art to women. This has made Tagore songs an essential part of life of the Bengalis who sing them in happiness, in distress, and at work.

Rabindranath once said that a song begins where a poem ends and that the message of music travels further than that of words. He used to ride on the wings of music in utter delight to spread his ideals, something he also did through his poems.

Visva-Bharati has so far published 63 volumes of *Gitabitan*, arranging the Tagore songs in alphabetical order with notations. A few more volumes remain to be published. [Sanjida Khatun]

Rabindra-Sangeet as a Resource for Indian Classical Bandishes

Rabindranath's titanic intellect found manifestation in almost every facet of fine art. One of the most outstanding amongst them is Rabindra-sangeet, which embodies a breathtaking fusion of his musicianship and poetic genius. Such was the impact of this creation, that it not only withstood the test of time for more than a century, but also secured a unique place for itself in the subcontinent's musical culture.

The objective of this article is not to deliberate on the beauty and depth of Rabindra-sangeet. There are countless works in this regard by people far more knowledgeable on Rabindranath and Rabindra-sangeet, and the influence of Classical music on Rabindra Sangeet has been amply analyzed and now stands as an accepted fact. What this article aims to focus on, is how and to what extent has Rabindra-sangeet, in its turn, influenced the more traditional forms of music and its exponents. In particular, there has been a pronounced influence of Rabindra-sangeet on some of the noted classical instrumentalists of North India. There are indeed scopes of debate over the rationale and the extent of potential of this influence, but the fact remains that it cannot be denied. There are far too many precedents in its favor.

In the succeeding sections of this article, it has been attempted to investigate, what elements in Rabindra-sangeet triggered this kind of influence on Indian Classical instrumentalists and what consequences it led to.

Traditional Elements in Rabindra-sangeet: It is an accepted fact that elements of Indian classical music have been used in an extremely intelligent and effective fashion in Rabindra-sangeet. It is indeed one of its most significant features. The application of this ingredient was however dictated principally by the perceived requirements of the mood evoked in the song, which was after all the core entity of his creation. An overt application of elements derived from classical music would have conflicted with this requirement. Therefore the application of classical elements, more often than not, had been subtle, and only to the extent necessary to express the emotive content of the song. Many of his songs therefore have only a partial conformity to ragas.

Of course, in cases where he found the tonal color of the raga in almost total conformity to the sentiment of the song, he adopted the raga in its entirety. On certain instances, we even see authentic classical compositions adopted faithfully in respect of both melody and rhythm, set to outstanding Bengali lyric. The urge to evoke a particular mood to his own satisfaction, often led him to blend ragas in unexpectedly beautiful and interesting ways, or to look for uncharted and unexplored nuances within the known frameworks of ragas. It was on these occasions that some of his most beautiful and intellectually challenging creations came forth.

The influence of Rabindra-sangeet on Indian classical Instrumental music is perhaps due to the fact that much of what is played on Indian classical instruments today is derived from vocal music, principally of classical as also to some extent, of non classical origin (like lighter variety of compositions derived from folk music such as *Kirtan* or *Bhatiyali*). Classical instrumentalists have always looked for newer ideas and inspirations to feed their imagination not merely from these sources. Rabindra-sangeet with its sheer beauty and lyricism combined with the exquisite embodiment of the classical genre, naturally turns out to be a very potential resource to prospect.

Influence of Rabindra sangeet on Classical Instruments and Instrumentalists.

The Beginning: The pioneering example in this regard was set by none other than the great Ustad Vilayat Khan Sahib. He had adopted the famous song, *Bhenge Mor Gharer Chabi,* into a beautiful, lilting light-classical composition. This was an interesting instance of a distinguished classical musician being motivated to imbibe the beauty and lyricism in Rabindra-sangeet .

The next example in this regard was set by Sri Buddhadev Dasgupta, the renowned sarodiya. Being a person with cultural roots in Bengal, he might have had a greater exposure to Rabindra-sangeet in general. His approach towards adoption of Rabindra-sangeet to classical music, naturally, was a more involved one. Out of the numerous classical compositions he has derived so far from Rabindra Sangeet, there are examples of transformations inspired by a variety of different aspects such as melodic appeal, interesting and unexpected application of raga movements, interesting ways of blending of ragas and even re-discovery of old classical compositions. His work in this area is based on years of exhaustive study and research in collaboration with Rabindra-sangeet experts like Shubhash Chowdhury.

The introduction of these kind of compositions in the arena of authentic Indian Classical Music took place over the decades of sixties and seventies. The initiation had been cautious and measured, considering the conventional mind-set of most of the contemporary musicians and listeners. For example, Sri Dasgupta played his first sarod composition, derived from the

Rabindrasageet *Shedin dujone*, in his AIR National Program in 1978, dubbing it as a "light classical composition set to Pilu" and not as "a sarod gat based on Rabindra Sangeet".

The Endeavor and its Acceptance: It took quite some time for this novel approach to be accepted by the musicians, critics and listeners in its correct perspective. At the initial stage, presentation of such compositions were limited to more intimate gatherings rather than important and full fledged classical concerts. The response of the musical community, though not of outright rejection was somewhat confused. On one hand they were moved by the aesthetic appeal of the compositions, but on the other, were not quite sure of the categorization of such compositions. These compositions were definitely not like light classical compositions (commonly termed as "*dhun*"). Their appeal was definitely more dignified, and were set to purer forms of Ragas for the *Dhuns* are mostly set to lighter and blended Ragas with an ambience akin to that of folk music.

They could also not be classified as authentic classical compositions or *bandishes* propagated over musical generations, as their origin was quite different. Sometimes they were sweepingly described as "Rabindra-sangeet played on sarod". This was a totally inappropriate description as well, as the compositions, more often than not, were quite different in their overall melodic construction, rythmic orientation and tempo than the original Rabindra-sangeet it had been derived from. In most cases the similarity was at a much more abstract level of melodic ideas and movements.

Therefore it was left to the proponents of this approach to educate and appraise the audience over the true characteristic of these compositions. This led to the formulation of certain experimental presentations featuring exponents of Rabindra-sangeet and classical musicians on a common stage, where some selected songs were presented along with their transformed versions of instrumental composition (or "*gat*" in the parlance of Hindusthani music), with adequate explanations in between. One of the earliest presentations of this kind was featured by Doordarshan Kendra, Calcutta with Budhhadev

Dasgupta, V.Balsara (the famous pianist and film music personality) and Sri Ramanuj Dasgupta, (one of the contemporary upcoming Rabindra Sangeet singers).

The reception to this program was very positive. Noted personalities from the sphere of Rabindra-sangeet as well as classical music acclaimed the effort. Further, as an interesting spin off, a large section of lay music-lovers and Tagore enthusiasts found an interesting cue towards the so-called "abstract" appeal of classical music. A number of similar experimental programs were staged over the following years, with other eminent personalities from spheres of classical music and Rabindra-sangeet, volunteering to take part in such ventures.

There have been quite a few presentations of these nature featuring Suchitra Mitra and Budhhadev Dasgupta, Subinoy Roy, Ravi Kichlu and Jaya Biswas and many others. Programs on this theme were accepted and presented by the AIR and Doordarshan on a number of occasions as well. Following suit, the Sangeet Natak Academy also funded a complete project on this theme. From this point onwards, it can be said, that the endeavor received its formal acceptance from the connoisseurs and listeners of classical music as also from the mass media. The idea was thereafter emulated by some of the most well known classical instrumentalists like Ustad Amjad Ali Khan. The trend continues to this day with dedicated stage programs focusing on classical compositions derived from Rabindra-sangeet. The interesting thing to note here is that just as the stage is shared by Rabindra-sangeet singers and classical instrumentalists, the galleries as well are shared by listeners of Rabindra-sangeet and classical music.

The Aspects of Transformation: Having delineated the course of evolution of this interesting work, it would be worthwhile to take a closer look at the aspects of transformation that it involves. Since this has to be examined on the basis of concrete examples, the author has chosen a few, from the works of Sri Budhhadev Dasgupta, whose contribution in this regard has not only been a pioneering one, but perhaps also the most profound and exhaustive. The compositions derived by him had been based on a number of different perspectives of musical thinking.

It should be borne in mind that when we talk of transformation, we are obviously not talking about simply playing Rabindra-sangeet on sarod. Certain ideas are taken from the original Rabindra-sangeet and used to formulate a composition suitable for the context of a classical instrument. The original song therefore, undergoes a change or a sort of reconstruction in that certain salient ideas taken from the song are represented using the elements of sarod vocabulary. The resulting composition can consequently differ to a considerable extent from the orginal song that inspired its creation. The difference mostly is on counts of rhythmic construction or tempo but sometimes also in details of melodic construction. The similarity on the other hand is rather abstract and more often than not at the level of an overall melodic outline. There are a few examples of course, where the nature of the original song itself is so akin to that of a classical presentation that it finds its way almost unaltered into a classical composition.

Revisiting Lost Domains in Ragas or Ragas Themselves: As mentioned before, in many of his creations Rabindranath had focused on ragas from rather striking and unexpected perspectives. Some of the movements he had used, though unusual, could not be challenged on counts of beauty and conformity to the raga. Some of these movements were taken from very old and traditional conventions in classical music. One such example is the use of R, G, M, P, D.., M G in the opening lines of *Shanti karo borishono*, based on Rag Tilak Kamod. From this took birth a beautiful, medium tempo (Madhya Laya) sarod composition (gat). An almost forgotten but exceedingly lyrical and romantic usage of Komal Gandhar in the latter part of the opening stanza (sthayee) of the song *Oi Janalar dhare* (Click here for an excerpt of the song or the *bandish* (Singer: Aniruddha Sinha; Ensemble: Sitar - Sugata Nag, Rahul Chatterjee, Sarod - Anirban Dasgupta, Pratyush Banerjee) is another outstanding example of such an application. In *Emono dine tare bola jai* we find a beautiful yet unconventional portrayal of Desh Malhar. Both of these songs have inspired excellent sarod gats set to teental. In some of the songs there has been an excellent delineation of uncommon Ragas. *Aji jato tara tabo akashe* (Excerpts: of the song or sarod-solo *bandish*. Artists: Sriradha Banerjee, sarod solo: Buddhadev Dasgupta) beautifully pictures Manjh Khambaj, a Raga which existed in the days of yore, but was somewhat rarely heard in the arena of pure classical music.

This song was almost completely imbibed into an excellent slow teental (Vilambit) composition by Buddhadev, and has been rendered by him in many of his important concerts. (Excerpt: Anirban Dasgupta, Buddhadev Dasgupta and Zakir Hussain playing Manjh Khamaj at Vassar College, Poughkeepsie, 1985.) Incidentally, the same raga which Tagore so adeptly applied in his song, was later revived and popularised in the world of classical music by Acharya Alauddin Khan and his son, Ustad Ali Akbar Khan, the legendary sarodiya.

Beauty of Approach, Movement and Melody: As mentioned before, many of the songs, have such a poignant and emotionally moving representation of commonly known ragas, that it would become rather difficult for a sensitive classical musician to overlook their intrinsic musicality. This poignancy or musicality in more objective terms can be interpreted as interesting application of note sequences. Many of the derived sarod compositions have been inspired by this factor. For example, in the song *Shedin dujone* one finds such an entrancing portrayal of the raga Pilu; here the notes of this rather common raga have been played with creative mastery.

This was, in fact, Budhadev's first inspiration to derive a sarod composition from Rabindra sangeet. In "*Chokhe-r aaloey*" one finds a simple yet serenely beautiful depiction of Yaman Kalyan. This was converted into a medium tempo composition set to Teen tal. A scintillating fast Tintal composition of Khambaj was created from *Amar kantha hote gaan ke nilo*. The rhythm of the original song (Dadra) had to be entirely changed in order to adapt it to the ambience of an instrumental presentation. This was necessary as the idea was to present not just the song but a full-fledged classical composition derived out of it. The basis of this transformation was the beauty of the melodic outline of the song. In contrast, *Jodi e amaro* is a striking example where not only is the melodic construction but also the rhythmic framework has been followed in to-to in the derived instrumental composition based on raga Kafi. Here as well, Tagore entrances us with the rare, beautiful yet unmistakable approach to Kafi starting from the note *Dhaibat.* Out of Tagore's many songs based on Bhairabi, *Tabo daya* is one of the most outstanding considering the exquisite application of notes the heightens the expression of beauty and devotion. This prompted the creation of a medium tempo gat, largely maintaining the note sequences but changing the rhythmic framework to the somewhat-more-brisk Teen tal. There are more examples of this nature, such as *Shey kon boner horin* (Hemant) vocal [by Agnibha Banerjee] or instrumental *bandish* [by the "Ensemble"}, or *Shopney amar mone holo* (Hameer). vocal [by Aniruddha Sinha] or instrumental *bandish* [composed by the "Ensemble"].

(Re)Discovering Old Classical Compositions: Most of the songs composed by Rabindranath are characterised by their outstanding individuality, both from the point of views of lyric and melody. But on a certain instances we also find him faithfully adapting the melodic content of old classical compositions. In certain cases where he found the melodic as well as rhythmic orientation of existing or old classical compositions in keeping with the clime of the song being composed he never hesitated to follow them with complete faith. It was perhaps his tribute to a rich tradition of classical music. Hence in some of the songs like *Shukho hin nishi din*, (vocal [by Haimanti Shukla], sarod *bandish* [by Buddhadev Dasgupta] or *Shunyo hate phiri he* we find priceless classical *bandishes,* faithfully captured and set to outstanding poetry. Even playing these songs verbatim on an instrument would make them sound like authentic classical instrumental compositions. An interesting commentary on this is provided in the audio-cassette series named "Rupantori", featuring stalwarts like Subinoy Roy and Prasun Banerjee.

Highlighting Tagore's Outstanding Ideations on Blending Ragas: Sometimes, his flights of imagination had led Tagore to such emotional moods, that the tonal colors available from the basic ragas were not adequate to express them. Under such circumstances he used his artistic liberty to blend ragas. This resulted in masterful combination of some of the known ragas producing unforeseen melodic shades of the highest artistic order.

One sees such a marriage between the ragas Todi and Bhairvi in the song *Rajani-r shesh tara*. Another unparalleled confluence of Bahar and Basant is noted in the song *Ami tomari shonge* (vocal [by Sriradha Banerjee] or *bandish* [by Buddhadev Dasgupta]). There may be many more examples. However, in the context of this discussion, it can be mentioned that both of these songs have provided potent ideas not only towards framing beautiful *bandishes* but also creating new kinds of blended ragas.

What it Means for a Classical Instrumentalist: Evolution of new ideas in the realm of classical instrumental music inspired by Rabindra-sangeet is of more than incidental significance to some classical instrumentalists. An instrumentalist who has experienced, understood the classical appeal in Rabindra Sangeet and has succeeded in deriving useful ideas from it will obviously find his musical horizon widening much more than ever before. He will develop the insight to discover interesting and unknown corners of known ragas, which will not only apply to the derived compositions but also to the more conventional aspects of his playing like Alap and Vistar. At a more abstract level it might also have significant effects and possibly improvements on his perspective of thinking on ragas. The derived compositions, which as metioned before, have a very distinctive aesthetic ambience would considerably expand his repertoire. He will find himself in possession the magic key to an inexhaustible repository of ideas.

Conclusion: It is a known fact that classical musicians over all ages and centuries have derived musical ideas from classical as well as non-classical sources. In a sense, therefore, this example of Rabindra-sangeet inspiring creation of classical compositions may be interpreted as a repetition of history.

However, a closer look suggests a difference. This lies in the artistic maturity of the source material in this case, so that a strong temptation to plagiarize must be resisted and the essence gleaned, and this can be an extremely challenging task.

Also, this endeavour has encouraged an interesting cross-influence. Some of the classical musicians have come down from their ivory towers and given Rabindra-sangeet its much overdue recognition. The exponents of Rabindra-sangeet by and large have welcomed this dialogue between these two islands of India's musical culture which were so far largely isolated from each other. For classical instrumentalists it opened up an extremely potent resource to excavate for newer ideas which are applicable to their own realm. Finally, the subtle yet long-term consequence could be to motivate future generations of musicians to enrich the realm of Classical Music from similar sources beyond the boundary their own domain

●●●

5

Selected Quotations of Rabindranath Tagore

A dewdrop is a perfect integrity that has no filial memory of its parentage.

A mind all logic is like a knife all blade. It makes the hand bleed that uses it.

According to the true Indian view, our consciousness of the world, merely as the sum total of things that exist, and as governed by laws, is imperfect. But it is perfect when our consciousness realizes all things as spiritually one with it, and therefore capable of giving us joy.

For us the highest purpose of this world is not merely living in it, knowing it and making use of it, but realizing our own selves in it through expansion of sympathy; not alienating ourselves from it and dominating it, but comprehending and uniting it with ourselves in perfect union.

All men have poetry in their hearts, and it is necessary for them, as much as possible, to express their feelings. For this they must have a medium, moving and pliant, which can refreshingly become their own, age after age. All great languages undergo change.

Those languages which resist the spirit of change are doomed and will never produce great harvests of thought and literature. When forms become fixed, the spirit either weakly accepts its imprisonment or rebels. All revolutions consists of the "within" fighting against invasion from "without"... All great human movements are related to some great idea.

Asks the Possible of the Impossible, "Where is your dwelling-place?" "In the dreams of the Impotent," comes the answer.

Beauty is in the ideal of perfect harmony which is in the universal being; truth the perfect comprehension of the universal mind. We individuals approach it through our own mistakes and blunders, through our accumulated experience, through our illumined consciousness - how, otherwise, can we know truth?

Beauty is truth's smile when she beholds her own face in a perfect mirror.

Bigotry tries to keep truth safe in its hand with a grip that kills it.

Children are living beings - more living than grown-up people who have built shells of habit around themselves. Therefore it is absolutely necessary for their mental health and development that they should not have mere schools for their lessons, but a world whose guiding spirit is personal love.

Death is not extinguishing the light; it is putting out the lamp because the dawn has come.

Do not say, "It is morning," and dismiss it with a name of yesterday. See it for the first time as a newborn child that has no name.

Everything comes to us that belongs to us if we create the capacity to receive it.

Facts are many, but the truth is one.

For the current of our spiritual life creeds, rituals and channels that may thwart or help, according to their fixity or openness. When a symbol or spiritual idea becomes rigidly elaborate in its construction, it supplants the idea which it should support.

Gross utility kills beauty. We now have all over the world huge production of things, huge organizations, huge administrations of empire - all obstructing the path of life. Civilization is waiting for a great consummation, for an expression of its soul in beauty. This must be your contribution to the world.

He who wants to do good knocks at the gate; he who loves finds the gate open.

I have spent my days stringing and unstringing my instrument while the song I came to sing remains unsung.

I slept and dreamt that life was joy. I awoke and saw that life was service. I acted and behold, service was joy.

If anger be the basis of our political activities, the excitement tends to become an end in itself, at the expense of the object to be achieved. side issues then assume an exaggerated importance, and all gravity of thought and action is lost; such excitement is not an exercise of strength, but a display of weakness.

If lifeís journey be endless where is its goal? The answer is, it is everywhere. We are in a palace which has no end, but which we have reached. By exploring it and extending our relationship with it we are ever making it more and more our own. The infant is born in the same universe where lives the adult of ripe mind. But its position is not like a schoolboy who has yet to learn his alphabet, finding himself in a college class. The infant has it own joy of life because the world is not a mere road, but a home, of which it will have more and more as it grows up in wisdom. With our road that gain is at every step, for it is the road and the home in one; it leads us on yet gives us shelter.

If you shut your door to all errors truth will be shut out.

If you shut your door to all errors truth will be shut out.

In love all the contradiction of existence merge themselves and are lost. Only in love are unity and duality not at variance. Love must be one and two at the same time. Only love is motion and rest in one. Our heart ever changes its place till it finds love, and then it has its rest... Bondage and liberation are not antagonistic in love. for love is most free and at the same time most bound.

In our desire for eternal life we pray for an eternity of our habit and comfort, forgetting that immortality is in repeatedly transcending the definite forms of life in order to pursue the infinite truth of life.

In the dualism of death and life there is a harmony. We know that the life of a soul, which is finite in its expression and infinite in its principle, must go through the portals of death in its journey to realise the infinite. It is death which is monistic, it has no life in it. But life is dualistic; it has an appearance as well as truth; and death is that appearance, that maya, which is an inseparable companion to life.

In the night we stumble over things and become acutely conscious of their separateness, but the day reveals the unity which embraces them. And the man whose inner vision is bathed in consciousness at once realizes the spiritual unity which reigns over all racial differences, and his mind no longer stumbles over individual facts, accepting them as final. He realizes that peace is an inner harmony and not an outer adjustment, that beauty carries the assurance of our relationship to reality, which waits for its perfection in the response of our love.

Leave out my name from the gift if it be a burden, but keep my song.

Let the dead have the immortality of fame, but the living the immortality of love.

Let us not pray to be sheltered from dangers but to be fearless when facing them.

Life is given to us, we earn it by giving it.

Life is perpetually creative because it contains in itself that surplus which ever overflows the boundaries of the immediate time and space, restlessly pursuing its adventure of expression in the varied forms of self-realization.

Life, like a child, laughs, shaking its rattle of death as it runs.

Life's errors cry for the merciful beauty that can modulate their isolation into a harmony with the whole.

Love adorns itself; it seeks to prove inward joy by outward beauty.

Love does not claim possession, but gives freedom.

Love gives beauty to everything it touches. Not greed and utility; they produce offices, but not dwelling houses. To be able to love material things, to clothe them with tender grace, and yet not be attached to them, this is a great service. Providence expects that we should make this world our own, and not live in it as though it were a rented tenement. We can only make it our own through some service, and that service is to lend it love and beauty from our soul. Your own experience shows you the difference between the beautiful, the tender, the hospitable, and the mechanically neat and monotonously useful.

Love is an endless mystery, for it has nothing else to explain it.

Love is not a mere impulse, it must contain truth, which is law.

Love is the only reality and it is not a mere sentiment. It is the ultimate truth that lies at the heart of creation.

Love is the only reality and it is not a mere sentiment. It is the ultimate truth that lies at the heart of creation.

Loveís overbrimming mystery joins death and life. It has filled my cup of pain with joy.

Love's gift cannot be given, it waits to be accepted.

Man goes into the noisy crowd to drown his own clamour of silence.

Man has a fund of emotional energy which is not all occupied with his self-preservation. This surplus seeks its outlet in the creation of art, for manís civilization is built upon his surplus... In everyday life, when we are mostly moved by our habits, we are economical in our expression, for then our soul-consciousness is at its low level - it has just volume enough to guide on in accustomed grooves. But when our heart is fully awakened in love, or in other great emotions, our personality is in its flood-tide.

Manís abiding happiness is not in getting anything but in giving himself up to what is greater than himself, to ideas which are larger than his individual life, the idea of his country, of humanity, of God.

Manís cry is to reach his fullest expression.

Men are cruel, but Man is kind.

Music fills the infinite between two souls. This has been muffled by the mist of our daily habits.

Never be afraid of the moments - thus sings the voice of the ever-lasting.

Objects of knowledge maintain an infinite distance from us who are the knowers. For knowledge is not union. Therefore the further world of freedom awaits us there where we reach truth, not through feeling it by senses or knowing it by reason, but through union of perfect sympathy. Obstacles are necessary companions to expression, and we know that the positive element in language is not in its obstructiveness. Exclusively viewed from the side of the obstacle, nature appears inimical to the idea of morality. But if that were absolutely true, moral life could never come to exists. Life, moral or physical, is not a completed fact, but a continual process, depending for its movement upon two contrary forces, the force of resistance and that of expression. Dividing these forces into two mutually opposing principles does not help us, for the truth dwells not in the opposition but in its continual reconciliation.

Our creation is the modification of relationship.

Our nature is obscured by work done by the compulsion of want or fear. The mother reveals herself in the service of her children, so our true freedom is not the freedom *from* action but freedom *in* action, which can only be attained in the work of love.

Praise shames me, for I secretly beg for it.

Religion is not a fractional thing that can be doled out in fixed weekly or daily measures as one among various subjects in the school syllabus. It is the truth of our complete being, the consciousness of our personal relationship with the infinite; it is the true center of gravity of our life. This we can attain during our childhood by daily living in a place where the truth of the spiritual world is not obscured by a crowd of necessities assuming artificial importance; where life is simple, surrounded by fullness of leisure, by ample space and pure air and profound peace of nature; and where men live with a perfect faith in the eternal life before them.

Religion, like poetry, is not a mere idea, it is expression. The self-expression of God is in the endless variety of creation; and our attitude toward the Infinite Being must also in its expression have a variety of individuality ceaseless and unending. Those sects which jealously build their boundaries with too rigid creeds excluding all spontaneous movement of the living spirit may hoard their theology but they kill religion.

Science urges us to occupy by our mind the immensity of the knowable world; our spiritual teacher enjoins us to comprehend by our soul the infinite spirit which is in the depth of the moving and changing facts of the world; the urging of our artistic nature is to realize the manifestation of personality in the world of appearance, the reality of existence which is in harmony with the real within us. Where this harmony is not deeply felt, there we are aliens and perpetually homesick. For man by nature is an artist; he never receives passively and accurately in his mind a physical representation of things around him.

So our daily worship of God is not really the process of gradual acquisition of him, but the daily process of surrendering ourselves, removing all obstacles to union and extending our consciousness of him in devotion and service, in goodness and in love.... Thus to be conscious of being absolutely enveloped by Brahma is not an act of mere concentration of mind. It must be the aim of the whole of our life. In all our thoughts and deeds we must be conscious of the infinite.

That I exist is a perpetual surprise which is life.

That I exist is a perpetual surprise which is life.

The best of us still have our aspirations for the supreme goals of life, which is so often mocked by prosperous people who now control the world. We still believe that the world has a deeper meaning than what is apparent, and that therein the human soul finds its ultimate harmony and peace. We still know that only in spiritual wealth does civilization attain its end, not in a prolific production of materials, and not in the competition of intemperate power with power.

The butterfly counts not months but moments, and has time enough.

The butterfly counts not months but moments, and has time enough.

The child learns so easily because he has a natural gift, but adults, because they are tyrants, ignore natural gifts and say that children must learn through the same process that they learned by. We insist upon forced mental feeding and our lessons become a form of torture. This is one of manís most cruel and wasteful mistakes.

The current of the world has its boundaries, otherwise it could have no existence, but its purpose is not shown in the boundaries which restrain it, but in its movement, which is toward perfection. The wonder is not that there should be obstacles and sufferings in this world, but that there should be law and order, beauty and joy, goodness and love.

The emancipation of our physical nature is in attaining health, of our social being in attaining goodness, and of our self in attaining love.

The fish in the water is silent, the animals on the earth is noisy, the bird in the air is singing. But man has in him the silence of the sea, the noise of the earth and the music of the air.

The fundamental desire of life is the desire to exist.

The greed of gain has no time or limit to its capaciousness. Its one object is to produce and consume. It has pity neither for beautiful nature nor for living human beings. It is ruthlessly ready without a moment's hesitation to crush beauty and life out of them, molding them into money.

The higher nature in man always seeks for something which transcends itself and yet is its deepest truth; which claims all its sacrifice, yet makes this sacrifice its own recompense. This is manís dharma, manís religion, and manís self is the vessel which is to carry this sacrifice to the altar.

The man who aims at his own agrandisement underrates everything else.

The meaning of our self is not to be found in its separateness from God and others, but in the ceaseless realisation of yoga, of union.

The most important lesson that man can learn from his life is not that there *is* pain in this world, but that it depends upon him to turn it into good account, that it is possible for him to transmute it into joy... Manís freedom is never in being saved troubles, but it is the freedom to take trouble for his own good, to make the trouble an element in his joy... that in pain is symbolised the infinite possibility of perfection, the eternal unfolding of joy.

The newer people, of this modern age, are more eager to amass than to realize.

The object of education is to give man the unity of truth... I believe in a spiritual world - not as anything separate from this world - but as its innermost truth. With the breath we draw we must always feel this truth, that we are living in God. Born in this great world, full of the mystery of the infinite, we cannot accept our existence as a momentary outburst of chance drifting on the current of matter toward an eternal nowhere. We cannot look upon our lives as dreams of a dreamer who has no awakening in all time. We have a personality to which matter and force are unmeaning unless related to something infinitely personal, whose nature we have discovered, in some measure, in human love, in the greatness of the good, in the martyrdom of heroic souls, in the ineffable beauty of nature which can never be a mere physical fact nor anything but an expression of personality.

The picture of a flower in a botanical book is information; its mission ends with our knowledge. But in pure art it is a personal communication. And therefore until it finds its harmony in the depth of our personality it misses the mark. We can treat existence solely as a textbook furnishing us lessons, and we shall not be disappointed, but we know that there its mission does not end. For in our joy in it, which is an end in itself, we feel that it is a communication, the final response of our knowing but the response of our being.

The pious sectarian is proud because he is confident of his right of possession in God. The man of devotion is meek because he is conscious of Godís right of love over his life and soul. The object of our possession becomes smaller than ourselves, and without acknowledging it in so many words the bigoted sectarian has an implicit belief that God can be kept secured for certain individuals in a cage which is of their own make. In a similar manner the primitive races of men believe that their ceremonials have a magic influence upon their deities. Sectarianism is a perverse form of worldliness in the disguise of religion; it breeds a narrowness of heart in a greater measure than the cult of the world based upon material interest can ever do. For undisguised pursuit of self has its safety in openness, like filth exposed to the sun and air. But the self-magnification with its consequent lessening of God that goes on unchecked under the cover of sectarianism loses its chance of salvation because it defiles the very source of purity. The potentiality of perfection outweighs actual contradictions... Existence in itself is here to prove that it cannot be an evil.

The progress of our soul is like a perfect poem. It has an infinite idea which once realised makes all movements full of meaning and joy. But if we detach its movements from that ultimate idea, if we do not see the infinite rest and only see the infinite motion, then existence appears to us a monstrous evil., impetuously rushing towards an unending aimlessness.

The question why there is evil in existence is the same as why there is imperfection... But this is the real question we ought to ask: Is this imperfection the final truth, is evil absolute and ultimate?

The significance which is in unity is an eternal wonder.

The tendency in modern civilization is to make the world uniform... Let the mind be universal. The individual should not be sacrificed.

The water in a vessel is sparkling; the water in the sea is dark. The small truth has words which are clear; the great truth has great silence.

There are men whose idea of life is tactic, who long for its continuation after death only because of their wish for permanence and not perfection; they love to imagine that the things to which they are accustomed will persist for ever. They completely identify themselves in their minds with their fixed surroundings and with whatever they have gathered, and to have to leave these is death for them. They forget that the true meaning of living is outliving, it is ever growing out of itself.

There is a point where in the mystery of existence contradictions meet; where movement is not all movement and stillness is not all stillness; where the idea and the form, the within and the without, are united; where infinite becomes finite, yet not losing its infinity. If this meeting is dissolved, then things become unreal.

Things are distinct not in their essence but in their appearance; in other words, in their relation to one to whom they appear. This is art, the truth of which is not in substance or logic, but in expression. Abstract truth may belong to science and metaphysics, but the world of reality belongs to art. Things in which we do not take joy are either a burden upon our minds to be got rid of at any cost; or they are useful, and therefore in temporary and partial relation to us, becoming burdensome when their utility is lost; or they are like wandering vagabonds, loitering for a moment on the outskirts of our recognition, and then passing on. A thing is only completely our own when it is a thing of joy to us.

This is the ultimate end of man, to find the *One* which is in him; which is his truth, which is his soul; the key with which he opens the gate of the spiritual life, the heavenly kingdom.

Those institutions which are static in their nature raise walls of division; this is why, in the history of religions, priesthood has always maintained dissensions and hindered the freedom of man. But the principle of life unites, it deals with the varied, and seeks unity.

Time is a wealth of change, but the clock in its parody makes it mere change and no wealth.

To be outspoken is easy when you do not wait to speak the complete truth.

To understand anything is to find in it something which

is our own, and it is the discovery of ourselves outside us which makes us glad. This relation of understanding is partial, but the relation of love is complete. In love the sense of difference is obliterated and the human soul fulfills its purpose in perfection, transcending the limits of itself and reaching across the threshold of the infinite. Therefore love is the highest bliss that man can attain to, for through it alone he truly knows that he is more than himself, and that he is at one with the All.

Truth cannot afford to be tolerant where it faces positive evil.

Want of love is a degree of callousness; for love is the perfection of consciousness. We do not love because we do not comprehend, or rather we do not comprehend because we do not love. For love is the ultimate meaning of everything around us. It is not a mere sentiment; it is truth; it is the joy that is at the root of all creation.

We can look upon a road from two different points of view. One regards it as dividing us from the object of desire; in that case we count every step of our journey over it as something attained by force in the face of obstruction. The other sees it as the road which leads us to our destination; and as such is part of our goal. It is already the beginning of our attainment, and by journeying over it we can only gain that which in itself it offers to us.

We can make truth ours by actively modulating its interrelations. This is the work of art; for reality is not based in the substance of things but in the principle of relationship. Truth is the infinite pursued by metaphysics; fact is the infinite pursued by science, while reality is the definition of the infinite which relates truth to the person. Reality is human; it is what we are conscious of, by which we are affected, that which we express.

We come nearest to the great when we are great in humility.

We do not raise our hands to the void for things beyond hope.

We gain freedom when we have paid the full price for our right to live.

We live in this world when we love it.

"What is Art?" It is the response of manís creative soul to the call of the real.

Whatever we treasure for ourselves separates us from others; our possessions are our limitations.

When he has the power to see things detached from self-interest and from the insistent claims of the lust of the senses, then alone can he have the true vision of the beauty that is everywhere. Then only can he see that what is unpleasant to us is not necessarily unbeautiful, but has its beauty in truth.

When the heat and motion of blind impulses and passions distract it on all sides, we can neither give nor receive anything truly. But when we find our centre in our soul by the power of self-restraint, by the force that harmonises all warring elements and unifies those that are apart, then all our isolated impressions reduce themselves to wisdom, and all our momentary impulses of heart find their completion in love; then all the petty details of our life reveal an infinite purpose, and all our thoughts and deeds unite themselves inseparably in an internal harmony.

When we accept any discipline for ourselves, we try to avoid everything except that which is necessary for our purpose; it is this purposefulness, which belongs to the adult mind, that we force upon school children. We say, "Never keep your mind alert, attend to what is before you, what has been given you." This tortures the child because it contradicts natureís purpose, and nature, the greatest of all teachers, is thwarted at every step by the human teacher who believes in machine-made lessons rather than life lessons, so that the growth of the childís mind is not only injured, but forcibly spoiled. Children should be surrounded with the things of nature which have their own educational value. Their minds should be allowed to stumble upon and be surprised at everything that happens in todayís life; the new tomorrow will stimulate their attention with new facts of life.

When we rejoice in our fullness, then we can part with out fruits with joy.

Whenever our life is stirred by truth, it expresses energy and comes to be filled, as it were, with a creative ardor. This consciousness of the creative urge is evidence of the force of truth on our mind.

Your mission is proving that a love for the earth, and for the things of the earth, is possible without materialism, a love without greed... I entreat you not to be turned by the call of vulgar strength, of stupendous size, by the spirit of storage, by the multiplication of millions, without meaning and without end. Cherish the ideal of perfection, and to that, relate all your work and all your movements. Though you love the material things of earth, they will not hurt you and you will bring heaven to earth and soul into things.

More Quotes

According to the true Indian view, our consciousness of the world, merely as the sum total of things that exist, and as governed by laws, is imperfect. But it is perfect when our consciousness realizes all things as spiritually one with it, and therefore capable of giving us joy. For us the highest purpose of this world is not merely living in it, knowing it and making use of it, but realizing our own selves in it through expansion of sympathy; not alienating ourselves from it and dominating it, but comprehending and uniting it with ourselves in perfect union.

All men have poetry in their hearts, and it is necessary for them, as much as possible, to express their feelings. For this they must have a medium, moving and pliant, which can refreshingly become their own, age after age. All great languages undergo change. Those languages which resist the spirit of change are doomed and will never produce great harvests of thought and literature. When forms become fixed, the spirit either weakly accepts its imprisonment or rebels. All revolutions consists of the "within" fighting against invasion from "without"... All great human movements are related to some great idea.

Beauty is in the ideal of perfect harmony which is in the universal being; truth the perfect comprehension of the universal mind. We individuals approach it through our own mistakes and blunders, through our accumulated experience, through our illumined consciousness - how, otherwise, can we know truth?

Children are living beings - more living than grown-up people who have built shells of habit around themselves. Therefore it is absolutely necessary for their mental health and development that they should not have mere schools for their lessons, but a world whose guiding spirit is personal love.

Death belongs to life as birth does. The walk is in the raising of the foot as in the laying of it down.

Facts are many, but the truth is one.

For the current of our spiritual life creeds, rituals and channels that may thwart or help, according to their fixity or openness. When a symbol or spiritual idea becomes rigidly elaborate in its construction, it supplants the idea which it should support.

God finds himself by creating.

Gross utility kills beauty. We now have all over the world huge production of things, huge organizations, huge administrations of empire - all obstructing the path of life. Civilization is waiting for a great consummation, for an expression of its soul in beauty. This must be your contribution to the world.

He is neither manifest nor hidden, He is neither revealed nor unrevealed: there are no words to tell that which He is. He is without form, without quality, without decay.

He who wants to do good knocks at the gate; he who loves finds the gate open.

I believe that there is an ideal hovering over the earth, an ideal of that Paradise which is not the mere outcome of imagination, but the ultimate reality towards which all things are moving. I believe that this vision of Paradise is to be seen in the sunlight, and the green of the earth, in the flowing streams, in the beauty of springtime and the repose of a winter morning. Everywhere in this earth the spirit of Paradise is awake and sending forth its voice.

If anger be the basis of our political activities, the excitement tends to become an end in itself, at the expense of the object to be achieved. side issues then assume an exaggerated importance, and all gravity of thought and action is lost; such excitement is not an exercise of strength, but a display of weakness.

If I say that He is within me, the universe is ashamed; if I say that He is without me, it is falsehood.

If lifeís journey be endless where is its goal? The answer is, it is everywhere. We are in a palace which has no end, but which we have reached. By exploring it and extending our relationship with it we are ever making it more and more our own. The infant is born in the same universe where lives the adult of ripe mind. But its position is not like a schoolboy who has yet to learn his alphabet, finding himself in a college class. The infant has it own joy of life because the world is not a mere road, but a home, of which it will have more and more as it grows up in wisdom. With our road that gain is at every step, for it is the road and the home in one; it leads us on yet gives us shelter.

If you shut your door to all errors truth will be shut out.

In Art, man reveals himself and not his objects.

In love all the contradiction of existence merge themselves and are lost. Only in love are unity and duality not at variance. Love must be one and two at the same time. Only love is motion and rest in one. Our heart ever changes its place till it finds love, and then it has its rest... Bondage and liberation are not antagonistic in love. for love is most free and at the same time most bound.

In love all the contradictions of existence merge themselves and are lost. Only in love are unity and duality not at variance.

In love, at one of its poles you find the personal, at the other the impersonal. At one you have the positive assertion - Here I am; at the other the equally strong denial - I am not. Without this ego what is love? And again, with only this ego how can love be possible?

In our desire for eternal life we pray for an eternity of our habit and comfort, forgetting that immortality is in repeatedly transcending the definite forms of life in order to pursue the infinite truth of life.

In the dualism of death and life there is a harmony. We know that the life of a soul, which is finite in its expression and infinite in its principle, must go through the portals of death in its journey to realise the infinite. It is death which is monistic, it has no life in it. But life is dualistic; it has an appearance as well as truth; and death is that appearance, that maya, which is an inseparable companion to life.

In the night we stumble over things and become acutely conscious of their separateness, but the day reveals the unity which embraces them. And the man whose inner vision is bathed in consciousness at once realizes the spiritual unity which reigns over all racial differences, and his mind no longer stumbles over individual facts, accepting them as final. He realizes that peace is an inner harmony and not an outer adjustment, that beauty carries the assurance of our relationship to reality, which waits for its perfection in the response of our love. It is our desires that limit the scope of our self-realisation, hinder our extension of consciousness, and give rise to sin, which is the innermost barrier that keeps us apart from our God, setting up disunion and arrogance of exclusiveness. For sin is not one mere action, but it is an attitude of life which takes for granted that our goal is finite, that our self is the ultimate truth, and that we are not all essentially one but exist each for his own separate individual existence.

Life is perpetually creative because it contains in itself that surplus which ever overflows the boundaries of the immediate time and space, restlessly pursuing its adventure of expression in the varied forms of self-realization.

Love adorns itself; it seeks to prove inward joy by outward beauty.

Love does not claim possession, but gives freedom.

Love gives beauty to everything it touches. Not greed and utility; they produce offices, but not dwelling houses. To be able to love material things, to clothe them with tender grace, and yet not be attached to them, this is a great service. Providence expects that we should make this world our own, and not live in it as though it were a rented tenement. We can only make it our own through some service, and that service is to lend it love and beauty from our soul. Your own experience shows you the difference between the beautiful, the tender, the hospitable, and the mechanically neat and monotonously useful.

Love is not a mere impulse, it must contain truth, which is law.

Loveís overbrimming mystery joins death and life. It has filled my cup of pain with joy.

Man has a fund of emotional energy which is not all occupied with his self-preservation. This surplus seeks its outlet in the creation of art, for manís civilization is built upon his surplus... In everyday life, when we are mostly moved by our habits, we are economical in our expression, for then our soul-consciousness is at its low level - it has just volume enough to guide on in accustomed grooves. But when our heart is fully awakened in love, or in other great emotions, our personality is in its flood-tide.

Manís abiding happiness is not in getting anything but in giving himself up to what is greater than himself, to ideas which are larger than his individual self, the idea of his country, of humanity, of God.

Manís abiding happiness is not in getting anything but in giving himself up to what is greater than himself, to ideas which are larger than his individual life, the idea of his country, of humanity, of God.

Manís cry is to reach his fullest expression.

Men are cruel, but Man is kind.

Music fills the infinite between two souls. This has been muffled by the mist of our daily habits.

Music is the purest form of art... therefore true poets, they who are seers, seek to express the universe in terms of music... The singer has everything within him. The notes come out from his very life. They are not materials gathered from outside. His idea and his expression are brother and sister; very often they are born as twins. In music the heart reveals itself immediately; it suffers not from any barrier of alien material. Therefore though music has to wait for its completeness like any other art, yet at every step it gives out the beauty of the whole. As the material of expression even words are barriers, for their meaning has to be construed by thought. But music never has to depend upon any obvious meaning; it expresses what no words can ever express.

What is more, music and the musician are inseparable. When the singer departs, his singing dies with him; it is in eternal union with the life and joy of the master. This world song is never for a moment separated from its singer. It is not fashioned from any outward material. It is his joy itself taking never-ending form. It is the great heart sending the tremor of its thrill over the sky. There is a perfection in each individual strain of this music, which is the revelation of completion in the incomplete. No one of its notes is final, yet each reflects the infinite. What does it matter if we fail to derive the exact meaning of this great harmony? Is it not like the hand meeting the string and drawing out at once all its tones at the touch? It is the language of beauty, the caress, that comes from the heart of the world and straightway reaches our heart. Last night, in the silence which pervaded the darkness, I stood alone and heard the voice of the singer of eternal melodies. When I went to sleep I closed my eyes with this last thought in mind, that even when I remain unconscious in slumber the dance of life will still go on in the hushed arena of my sleeping body, keeping step wit the stars. The heart will throb, the blood will leap in the veins, and the millions of living atoms of my body will vibrate in tune with the note of the harp-string that thrills at the touch of the master.

Nationality is respectable only when it is on the defence, when it is waging wars of liberation it is sacred; when those of domination it is accursed.

Never be afraid of the moments - thus sings the voice of the ever-lasting.

Objects of knowledge maintain an infinite distance from us who are the knowers. For knowledge is not union. Therefore the further world of freedom awaits us there where we reach truth, not through feeling it by senses or knowing it by reason, but through union of perfect sympathy.

Obstacles are necessary companions to expression, and we know that the positive element in language is not in its obstructiveness. Exclusively viewed from the side of the obstacle, nature appears inimical to the idea of morality. But if that were absolutely true, moral life could never come to exists. Life, moral or physical, is not a completed fact, but a continual process, depending for its movement upon two contrary forces, the force of resistance and that of expression. Dividing these forces into two mutually opposing principles does not help us, for the truth dwells not in the opposition but in its continual reconciliation.

Our creation is the modification of relationship.

Our nature is obscured by work done by the compulsion of want or fear. The mother reveals herself in the service of her children, so our true freedom is not the freedom *from* action but freedom *in* action, which can only be attained in the work of love.

Religion is not a fractional thing that can be doled out in fixed weekly or daily measures as one among various subjects in the school syllabus. It is the truth of our complete being, the consciousness of our personal relationship with the infinite; it is the true center of gravity of our life. This we can attain during our childhood by daily living in a place where the truth of the spiritual world is not obscured by a crowd of necessities assuming artificial importance; where life is simple, surrounded by fullness of leisure, by ample space and pure air and profound peace of nature; and where men live with a perfect faith in the eternal life before them.

Religion, like poetry, is not a mere idea, it is expression. The self-expression of God is in the endless variety of creation; and our attitude toward the Infinite Being must also in its expression have a variety of individuality ceaseless and unending. Those sects which jealously build their boundaries with too rigid creeds excluding all spontaneous movement of the living spirit may hoard their theology but they kill religion.

Science urges us to occupy by our mind the immensity of the knowable world; our spiritual teacher enjoins us to comprehend by our soul the infinite spirit which is in the depth of the moving and changing facts of the world; the urging of our artistic nature is to realize the manifestation of personality in the world of appearance, the reality of existence which is in harmony with the real within us. Where this harmony is not deeply felt, there we are aliens and perpetually homesick. For man by nature is an artist; he never receives passively and accurately in his mind a physical representation of things around him.

So our daily worship of God is not really the process of gradual acquisition of him, but the daily process of surrendering ourselves, removing all obstacles to union and extending our consciousness of him in devotion and service, in goodness and in love.... Thus to be conscious of being absolutely enveloped by Brahma is not an act of mere concentration of mind. It must be the aim of the whole of our life. In all our thoughts and deeds we must be conscious of the infinite.

Taking shelter in the dead is death itself, and only taking all the risk of life to the fullest extent is living.

That I exist is a perpetual surprise which is life.

The best of us still have our aspirations for the supreme goals of life, which is so often mocked by prosperous people who now control the world. We still believe that the world has a deeper meaning than what is apparent, and that therein the human soul finds its ultimate harmony and peace. We still know that only in spiritual wealth does civilization attain its end, not in a prolific production of materials, and not in the competition of intemperate power with power.

The butterfly counts not months but moments, and has time enough.

The child learns so easily because he has a natural gift, but adults, because they are tyrants, ignore natural gifts and say that children must learn through the same process that they learned by. We insist upon forced mental feeding and our lessons become a form of torture. This is one of manís most cruel and wasteful mistakes.

The current of the world has its boundaries, otherwise it could have no existence, but its purpose is not shown in the boundaries which restrain it, but in its movement, which is toward perfection. The wonder is not that there should be obstacles and sufferings in this world, but that there should be law and order, beauty and joy, goodness and love. The emancipation of our physical nature is in attaining health, of our social being in attaining goodness, and of our self in attaining love.

The fundamental desire of life is the desire to exist.

The higher nature in man always seeks for something which transcends itself and yet is its deepest truth; which claims all its sacrifice, yet makes this sacrifice its own recompense. This is manís dharma, manís religion, and manís self is the vessel which is to carry this sacrifice to the altar.

The highest education is that which does not merely give us information but makes our life in harmony with all existence.

The man who aims at his own agrandisement underrates everything else.

The man whose acquaintance with the world does not lead him deeper than science leads him, will never understand what it is that the man with the spiritual vision finds in these natural phenomena. The water does not merely cleanse his limbs, but it purifies his heart; for it touches his soul. The earth does not merely hold his body, but it gladdens his mind; for its contact is more than physical contact, it is a living presence. When a man does not realise his kinship with the world, he lives in a prison-house whose walls are alien to him When he meets the eternal spirit in all objects, then is he emancipated, for then he discovers the fullest significance of the world into which he is born; then he finds himself in perfect truth, and his harmony with the All is established.

The meaning of our self is not to be found in its separateness from God and others, but in the ceaseless realisation of yoga, of union.

The most important lesson that man can learn from his life is not that there *is* pain in this world, but that it depends upon him to turn it into good account, that it is possible for him to transmute it into joy... Maní́s freedom is never in being saved troubles, but it is the freedom to take trouble for his own good, to make the trouble an element in his joy... that in pain is symbolised the infinite possibility of perfection, the eternal unfolding of joy. The object of education is to give man the unity of truth. Formerly, when life was simple, all the different elements of man were in complete harmony. But when there came the separation of the intellect from the spiritual and the physical, the school education put entire emphasis on intellect and the physical side of man. We devote our sole attention to giving children information, not knowing that by this emphasis we are accentuating a break between the intellectual, physical, and the spiritual life.

The object of education is to give man the unity of truth... I believe in a spiritual world - not as anything separate from this world - but as its innermost truth. With the breath we draw we must always feel this truth, that we are living in God. Born in this great world, full of the mystery of the infinite, we cannot accept our existence as a momentary outburst of chance drifting on the current of matter toward an eternal nowhere. We cannot look upon our lives as dreams of a dreamer who has no awakening in all time. We have a personality to which matter and force are unmeaning unless related to something infinitely personal, whose nature we have discovered, in some measure, in human love, in the greatness of the good, in the martyrdom of heroic souls, in the ineffable beauty of nature which can never be a mere physical fact nor anything but an expression of personality.

The picture of a flower in a botanical book is information; its mission ends with our knowledge. But in pure art it is a personal communication. And therefore until it finds its harmony in the depth of our personality it misses the mark. We can treat existence solely as a textbook furnishing us lessons, and we shall not be disappointed, but we know that there its mission does not end. For in our joy in it, which is an end in itself, we feel that it is a communication, the final response of our knowing but the response of our being.

The pious sectarian is proud because he is confident of his right of possession in God. The man of devotion is meek because he is conscious of Godís right of love over his life and soul. The object of our possession becomes smaller than ourselves, and without acknowledging it in so many words the bigoted sectarian has an implicit belief that God can be kept secured for certain individuals in a cage which is of their own make. In a similar manner the primitive races of men believe that their ceremonials have a magic influence upon their deities. Sectarianism is a perverse form of worldliness in the disguise of religion; it breeds a narrowness of heart in a greater measure than the cult of the world based upon material interest can ever do. For undisguised pursuit of self has its safety in openness, like filth exposed to the sun and air. But the self-magnification with its consequent lessening of God that goes on unchecked under the cover of sectarianism loses its chance of salvation because it defiles the very source of purity.

The potentiality of perfection outweighs actual contradictions... Existence in itself is here to prove that it cannot be an evil.

The progress of our soul is like a perfect poem. It has an infinite idea which once realised makes all movements full of meaning and joy. But if we detach its movements from that ultimate idea, if we do not see the infinite rest and only see the infinite motion, then existence appears to us a monstrous evil., impetuously rushing towards an unending aimlessness.

The revelment of the infinite in the finite, which is the motive of all creation, is not seen in its perfection in the starry heavens, in the beauty of the flowers. It is in the soul of man.

The same stream of life that runs through my veins night and day runs through the world and dances in rhythmic measures.

The significance which is in unity is an eternal wonder.

The tendency in modern civilization is to make the world uniform... Let the mind be universal. The individual should not be sacrificed. The touch of an infinite mystery passes over the trivial and the familiar, making it break out into ineffable music... The trees, the stars, and the blue hills ache with a meaning which can never be uttered in words. The tragedy of human life consists in our vain attempts to stretch the limits of things which can never become unlimited, to reach the infinite by absurdly adding to the rungs of the ladder of the finite.

There are men whose idea of life is tactic, who long for its continuation after death only because of their wish for permanence and not perfection; they love to imagine that the things to which they are accustomed will persist for ever. They completely identify themselves in their minds with their fixed surroundings and with whatever they have gathered, and to have to leave these is death for them. They forget that the true meaning of living is outliving, it is ever growing out of itself.

There is a moral law in this world which has its application both to individuals and organised bodies of men. You cannot go on violating these laws in the name of your nation, yet enjoy their advantage as individuals. We may forget truth for our convenience, but truth does not forget us. Prosperity cannot save itself without moral foundation. Until man can see the gaping chasm between his full storehouse and his humanity, until he can feel the unity of mankind, the kind of barbarism which you call civilisation will exist. There is a point where in the mystery of existence contradictions meet; where movement is not all movement and stillness is not all stillness; where the idea and the form, the within and the without, are united; where infinite becomes finite, yet not losing its infinity. If this meeting is dissolved, then things become unreal.

Things are distinct not in their essence but in their appearance; in other words, in their relation to one to whom they appear. This is art, the truth of which is not in substance or logic, but in expression. Abstract truth may belong to science and metaphysics, but the world of reality belongs to art.

This is the ultimate end of man, to find the *One* which is in him; which is his truth, which is his soul; the key with which he opens the gate of the spiritual life, the heavenly kingdom.

Those institutions which are static in their nature raise

walls of division; this is why, in the history of religions, priesthood has always maintained dissensions and hindered the freedom of man. But the principle of life unites, it deals with the varied, and seeks unity. Those who have everything but thee, my God, laugh at those who have nothing but thyself.

To understand anything is to find in it something which is our own, and it is the discovery of ourselves outside us which makes us glad. This relation of understanding is partial, but the relation of love is complete. In love the sense of difference is obliterated and the human soul fulfills its purpose in perfection, transcending the limits of itself and reaching across the threshold of the infinite. Therefore love is the highest bliss that man can attain to, for through it alone he truly knows that he is more than himself, and that he is at one with the All.

True modernism is freedom of mind, not slavery of taste. It is independence of thought and action, not tutelage under European schoolmasters. It is science but not its wrong application to life. Truth cannot afford to be tolerant where it faces positive evil.

Want of love is a degree of callousness; for love is the perfection of consciousness. We do not love because we do not comprehend, or rather we do not comprehend because we do not love. For love is the ultimate meaning of everything around us. It is not a mere sentiment; it is truth; it is the joy that is at the root of all creation.

We [poets] set men free from their desires.

We believe that mere movement is life, and that the more velocity it has, the more it expresses vitality.

We can look upon a road from two different points of view. One regards it as dividing us from the object of desire; in that case we count every step of our journey over it as something attained by force in the face of obstruction. The other sees it as the road which leads us to our destination; and as such is part of our goal. It is already the beginning of our attainment, and by journeying over it we can only gain that which in itself it offers to us.

●●●